THE ROLE OF THE SUPREME COURT IN AMERICAN POLITICAL CULTURE

The Role of the Supreme Court in American Political Culture

Preserving the Founding Myths

Kerry L. Hunter

The Edwin Mellen Press
Lewiston•Queenston•Lampeter

Library of Congress Cataloging-in-Publication Data

Hunter, Kerry L.
The role of the Supreme Court in American political culture : preserving the founding myths / Kerry L. Hunter.
p. cm.
Includes bibliographical references and index.
ISBN 0-7734-5843-3
I. Title.

hors série.

A CIP catalog record for this book is available from the British Library.

The Edwin Mellen Press
Box 450
Lewiston, New York
USA 14092-0450

The Edwin Mellen Press
Box 67
Queenston, Ontario
CANADA L0S 1L0

The Edwin Mellen Press, Ltd.
Lampeter, Ceredigion, Wales
UNITED KINGDOM SA48 8LT

Printed in the United States of America

For Chris Jones,

In appreciation of
your support and enthusiasm.

Table of Contents

Table of Illustrations

Preface

It is my pleasure to recommend this book, by my colleague and friend, Kerry Hunter. This book should be widely read by academics, students, and the general public. Its accessibility as well as its provocative argument will engage both the specialist and the layperson. This book comes at an opportune time as the country ponders the political implications of change in the personnel of the U.S. Supreme Court over the coming decade. Who will be appointed to the Court has become a major partisan political issue. Hunter presents a cogent argument that simultaneously offers a new understanding of the Supreme Court's unique role in the American constitutional system and a framework for a new theory of judicial review. This book will be a useful text in any number of academic courses in political science and legal studies. Besides those scholars and students who have an interest in the federal judiciary and constitutional law, this is an excellent book for those interested in American government, American political theory and in American political culture.

Hunter guides his audience, with accessible language and clarity of analysis, through a discussion of the underlying values that constitute American political culture. Next, he assesses the prevalent contemporary theories of judicial review. He argues that current liberal and conservative theories ultimately fail because they do not fully understand the relationship between the Supreme Court's unique role in the political process and the need to balance, preserve and sustain the complex and contradictory underlying values in American political culture. Finally, he presents the framework for an alternative theory of judicial review that is based on an understanding that the principle function of the Supreme Court is to preserve the mythical ideals of American political culture.

The underlying political values that collectively constitute American political culture are derived from many sources including classical liberalism, republicanism, and constitutional principles of separation of powers and federalism. Hunter demonstrates that imbedded within and between these sources are values that are contradictory yet collectively embraced by Americans as the foundations of individual liberty and democratic governance. Classical liberalism predicates individual liberty on the ideal of unalienable natural rights yet also calls for those rights to be constrained by the rule of government as determined by the majority; both government responsive to the will of the majority and individual liberty free from governmental control are ideals simultaneously embraced by Americans but in reality are often in contradiction. Similarly, Americans believe in majority rule but also the need for republican checks on the majority to protect individual rights. Americans simultaneously embrace state sovereignty yet also national unity. Americans distrust government officials, hence the value of separated powers, yet they also value the republican belief in the need for virtuous leaders. These contradictions are not a weakness. Instead, Hunter argues that the true genius, and durable strength, of the American political culture is its capacity to embrace all of these contradictions and yet act as if there are no contradictions. This then is the mythology of American political culture. It is this set of mythical values that distinguishes American democracy and that shapes our collective understanding of politics.

Hunter argues that the unique role of the U.S. Supreme Court in our constitutional system of government is the necessity of maintaining this mythology. While the Court is called upon to resolve cases involving these conflicting values it must do so in a manner that does not appear to resolve an issue once and for all, and, in a manner that pays respect to the importance of these contending values. Hunter writes, 'the Court's job is to keep juggling'. Besides respecting these contending values, the Court must also be cognizant of the political situation. Hunter argues that the Court loses its legitimacy when its actions appear to serve a primarily partisan political purpose. To illustrate this framework for a theory of judicial review, *Roe v. Wade* and *Bush v. Gore* are discussed as examples of where the Court's decision violated its mythical role and therefore subjected the Court to criticisms from both the liberal and conservative ends of the American political spectrum.

While the ideals that constitute American political culture are mythical the Supreme Court is asked to render decisions that translate myth into actual public policy. To do so, *requires the Court to play a political role.* Hunter argues that current theories of judicial review, whether they are espoused from the ideological Right – Bork, Scalia, Rehnquist, Ely – or from the ideological Left – Ackerman, Sunstein, or Dworkin – fail to consider the mythological function of the Court. Current theories do not recognize that their approach to judicial review is, in essence, validating one set of underlying values while discounting other underlying values. These theories of judicial review share the same flaw, that is, so long as the Court validates their underlying values it is not correctly "politicized". Hunter demonstrates that the Court's necessary political role is to avoid the trap of validating one underlying set of values in American political culture at the expense of other, equally embraced and cherished values. The long-term vitality of the American experiment in democracy depends on the Court understanding and protecting this mythical role.

Hunter concludes that it is also important that those who appoint and confirm judges to the Supreme Court appreciate the Court's unique place in the American constitutional system. The Court's exercise of judicial review is much greater than simply one of the many "checks and balances" between Congress, the executive branch and the judiciary; it is a power that when properly used sustains the vitality of the connected web of fundamental political values and ideals. It is these values and ideals that allow for American democracy to adapt to new circumstances. Conserving important ideals while simultaneously adapting those ideals to new conditions is one responsibility of the Court. As American society evolves, the Court's second duty is to recognize when the particular situation necessitates a new juggling or reordering of those values. Does recognition of these two purposes demand the appointment of virtuous and wise judges? Yes. But ultimately, of course, this recognition demands virtuous and wise citizens. It is the public's understanding of the Supreme Court's unique role that will ultimately determine the future success of American democracy. This book is an important contribution to that understanding.

Timothy D. Jeske
Political Science Department
Yakima Valley Community College

Acknowledgments

Thanks to Gene Place, Donita Christensen, and Neva Geisler for reading an extremely rough draft and providing many helpful comments. Thanks also to constitutional law students at Albertson College of Idaho for challenging my developing arguments. Special thanks go to Eric Spencer for a thorough final editing, and John Reuter for technical help and inspiration. Thanks also to Kristen Peters for her photographic skills, and Sam Hunter for his computer expertise. Finally thanks to Zach Hagadone of the *Sandpoint Reader* for the cover and political cartoons.

The Supreme Hijackers

Introduction

Though the phrase "constitutional crisis" was often used to describe the controversial Supreme Court decision that elevated George Bush Jr. to the American presidency, hindsight suggests that the Court's brief adventure in the election process neither weakened the viability of the Constitution nor jeopardized, even slightly, the Court's legitimacy. The Court promptly scurried behind their marbled walls and politics quickly went back to normal. And despite a few minor protests, the legitimacy of the Bush presidency was never seriously in doubt. In fact, by the time George Bush sought "re-election," Americans, with the exception of certain academics, seemed to have forgotten that we really did not know if he had ever been elected in the first place. Though this forgive-and-forgetfulness of the American voting public frustrates many who worry over the health of our democracy, it is possibly fortunate that in this instance the American public did forget.

Some might argue that to insure even minimum accountability, voters must at least recollect the most recent election, and that the failure to be vigilant in remembering the judicial activism that resulted in Bush's victory could lead to more of the same in the future. This argument makes some sense. Political apathy can lead to corruption and secret deals behind closed doors. But directing too much attention to Court activism could also be detrimental. A constitutional crisis might very well result if the American public ever becomes overly cynical about the Supreme Court's willingness to use political power.

Ever since the controversial *Marbury* v. *Madison* decision, when the Court first ruled an act of Congress to be unconstitutional, academics and politicians have debated the proper role of the non-elected Supreme Court in American democracy. What business does the Court have in overturning laws passed by the democratically elected Congress and thus making policy by default? Convinced that the Senate rejected his appointment to the high Court for political reasons, Judge Robert Bork has recently led a "conservative" attack on Court activism and the selection process.[1] Even more recently, "liberal"[2] Harvard Law professor Alan Dershowitz took up the charge by characterizing the Court as "hijacking" the election of 2000.[3]

These are legitimate concerns. A healthy democracy does require informed voters with memories. Moreover, a healthy democracy must be committed to the separation of powers and to the reluctance of the non-elected judiciary to make the law. Nevertheless, the following pages argue that much criticism of the Supreme Court has been misguided because the Supreme Court by necessity must fulfill more than a traditional judicial function in American politics. To be sure, the Court has made mistakes and both Bork and Dershowitz correctly perceive problems with the Court. But the direction of their criticism is off center. Not only is it absolutely necessary for the Supreme Court to be political, and thereby guilty of shaping policy on a regular basis, the Court's political role is *essential* in helping to preserve American democracy. American political ideals make powerful but inconsistent and ultimately impossible demands on government officials. Yet, it is imperative that Americans sincerely *believe* in the impossible, that we maintain a healthy faith in these ideals in spite of their multiple contradictions.

I ultimately want to refer to American idealism as mythical—a word I use with some trepidation. The word "myth" has developed negative connotations to the average American. For some, it suggests fantasy and wishful thinking, and

[1] See Robert H. Bork, *The Tempting of America: The Political Seduction of the Law*, (New York: The Free Press, 1990).
[2] As will become clear in reading this book, the labels liberal and conservative are problematic the way they are used in political discourse today. Hence the quotation marks.
[3] Alan M. Dershowitz, *Supreme Injustice: How the High Court Hijacked Election 2000,* (Oxford, New York: Oxford University Press 2001).

thus connotes a certain frivolity and lack of seriousness. But I believe that preserving American political mythology is serious business, perhaps the most serious business. We cannot prove, for example, that humans have a right to respect and freedom. We can passionately believe this, but such beliefs are impossible to prove in the way that we can potentially prove one's guilt or innocence. Most important American ideals are like this. We cannot prove that a person has the right to be considered innocent until proven guilty. Nor can we prove a right to free speech, freedom of religion, etc. These are beliefs, ideals, even wishful thinking. And though they are not verifiable facts, they do provide the central story by which our society makes sense of the world. They operate deep in our collective psyche and as powerful ideals can play a vital role in curbing excessive governmental interference in our lives. In the following pages I argue that the Supreme Court's unique position makes preserving these myths its essential function.

In 1955, historian Louis Hartz argued in *The Liberal Tradition in America,* that America's political culture was shaped almost exclusively by classic *liberal*[4] ideals. Though inaccessible to the casual reader, the Hartz thesis continues to be heavily debated by scholars of American political culture. Few question that *liberal* ideals are at the center of American political discourse. But understanding the full extent of their impact and importance requires continual re-examination. In Chapter One we enter that process and discover a richness of powerful but inconsistent ideals. It is suggested that this inconsistency is a peculiar strength of American democracy and that liberty depends on the constant friction between conflicting ideals. I also hint that the U.S. Supreme Court has a key political role in preserving a robust belief in these conflicting ideals—an argument that is not be fully developed until the final chapter.

---

[4] As an attempt at clarity, I will italicize *liberal* throughout the rest of the book when referring to classic *liberal* ideals as opposed to modern liberal political positions.

Where Chapter One focuses on *liberal* theory in general, Chapter Two examines the conflicting demands *liberal* ideals make on specific government institutions. *Liberalism* has a peculiar way of contemplating governmental powers—resulting in contradictory expectations of government institutions. As part of the judicial branch, the Supreme Court is expected to operate within the limits *liberal* ideals demand. When it is perceived as stepping outside of those boundaries it is understandably seen as courting a potential constitutional crisis. Nevertheless, I suggest that the health of the Constitution ultimately depends on an extra-constitutional Supreme Court capable of exercising a paternalistic responsibility of promoting *liberal* paradoxical mythology.

This leads us to Chapter Three, where we discover that Hartz told only half the story. To the extent that the Court, or any other government institution, is required to exercise paternal authority to promote *liberal* ideals, something other than *liberalism* must be at work. This Chapter examines the ideals of republicanism and their elitist distrust of democracy and direct opposition to the *liberal* ideals we explored in Chapters One and Two. Yet I argue that republican ideals are equally central and necessary to American political culture—making powerful demands of their own. In fact, though republican ideals contradict *liberalism*, they are actually necessary to maintain *liberal* freedoms. Again, the Supreme Court has a unique opportunity and obligation to promote healthy belief in these ideals.

Chapter Four takes us in a different direction by examining the major judicial philosophies of the day, liberal and conservative. In this chapter we discover that all who have thus far attempted to delineate a proper role for the Supreme Court in American democracy have failed to fully contemplate the Court's necessarily mythical role. That is, all fail to comprehend the Court's unique responsibility to promote and preserve the many contradictory ideals in American political culture.

Finally, Chapter Five explores this argument that the Court's essential role in the American system is the political role of preserving myth. First I examine two cases where I argue the Court failed to meet this most important responsibility. The first is *Roe* v. *Wade*, the Court's most controversial abortion case. Though *Roe* initially seemed a victory for women, close scrutiny suggests otherwise. Obviously, this argument will initially displease many people. And perhaps my willingness to take on this case proves that fools do indeed rush in where angels fear to tread. Nevertheless, I believe that regardless of one's position on a woman's right to medical self-determination, close examination of *Roe* v. *Wade* reveals a Court whose vision was far too narrow, a Court so anxious to step in and right self-evident wrongs that it forgets to preserve belief in American idealism. By throwing caution to the wind and openly entering the political fray over abortion, the Court exposed itself to the criticism that what mattered most were not American ideals but the ideals of those individuals in positions of power. This was a mistake and in making it the Court ultimately failed the nation. In fact, any time the Court encourages the perception that it is just another power institution willing to act outside the boundaries of ideals, groups like women, who have historically been out of power and therefore most dependant on idealism, have the most to lose.

The second case is *Bush* v. *Gore*, where the Court entangled itself in the 2000 presidential election. Once again I argue that in this case the Court failed all of us, even those who wanted George Bush to become the next president. As with *Roe*, the Court focused myopically on immediate concerns. When the Court's actions seem to promote partisan ideology, it greatly harms all of us by jeopardizing our belief in the importance of ideals. Ironically, in the *Bush* v. *Gore* case, the ideals of republicanism come under attack. True, the Republican Party does not limit itself to the ideals of republicanism, but to the extent that they want to encourage a belief in the necessity of virtuous leaders, they must discourage the perception that members of the Court are willing to use their positions of power to promote partisan or even personal political agendas.

We finally turn to *Brown* v. *Board of Education*, an extremely controversial case in which an activist Court successfully nudged the nation in a new direction while simultaneously meeting its more essential role of encouraging American idealism. In *Brown*, the Court controversially ruled that it was no longer constitutional for states to practice racial segregation in public schools. The Court was no less political in this ruling than it was in *Roe* v. *Wade* or *Bush* v. *Gore*, stepping right into the middle of a major political controversy. So why did it succeed in its essential role of preserving myth here and not in the other two instances? We examine the factors that made it so and suggest ways for politicians and justices to meet this most important obligation.

For those whose interests are directly affected, the Court's decisions surely have lasting and extremely significant results. Yet the implications of the Court's actions for the nation extend beyond determining who will be the next president, whether or not schools will be immediately de-segregated, or whether or not women will immediately be free to exercise the right to choose an abortion. Preserving any freedom requires preserving the force of ideals that limit those who exercise power. If anything, our history suggests that institutional balances of power alone are not enough to keep power from being monopolized and abused. If we ever stop believing that our ideals matter, we really will have a constitutional crisis. The Court can do much to help us keep that faith.

7

Partisan Polemics

Chapter One
Mythical Ideals In American Political Culture

Each election cycle, politicians and their supporters make Herculean efforts and spend millions of dollars trying to insure that their favorite party is in power in Washington D.C. Yet most Americans do not experience significant changes in their day-to-day lives with a change in the party controlling Congress or the presidency. In terms of actual policy, little separates the two major parties, as the drive to get elected moves both parties toward the center. For example, some consider Bill Clinton, with his emphasis on free trade and balanced budgets, to be the best Republican president in recent history. Similarly, Republican George Bush sounded very much like a Democrat with his "no child left behind" federal education mandates, protections for the American steel industry, and nation building in Iraq. Nevertheless, those actively engaged in the partisan struggle do feel like there is a tremendous amount at stake each election, and often feel an acute sense of impending doom when the rival party wins. If actual policy differences are not that significant, what explains this degree of partisan passion?

Clearly, part of this passion can be explained by pure self-interest. Many members of a candidate's election team hope to gain personally by securing positions in the administration of their candidate. Others realistically hope their particular economic or special interest will be supported more directly through the election of their candidate, and spend large sums of money with this thought in mind. However raw self-interest alone cannot explain the strong feelings at work in American political campaigns. Most voters will not experience a direct economic change due to the outcome of a national election. In fact, local leadership changes will affect most people's immediate economic situations more than national ones, yet Americans always turn out in the greatest numbers during a presidential election year. This suggests that something other than basic economic calculation is at work in the minds of most voters.

Not that economics do not matter. As candidates promising "no new taxes" clearly understand, Americans definitely go to the polls with their self-interests in mind. Nevertheless, the serious economic-self-interest-calculating voter could easily determine that it makes much more economic sense to purchase a lottery ticket than to vote for the president of the United States. In fact, the chances of one voter making a difference in a presidential race are so infinitesimally small, that only a fool would vote for purely self-interested reasons. But voters do not let such rational economic calculations govern their behavior. Voting, particularly in national and more particularly in presidential elections, is an emotional, patriotic act for most Americans, and patriotism appeals to abstract American mythical ideals more than to concrete economic self-interest.

Like advertisers of any commodity, campaign managers know this. They know that abstract ideals are much more valuable for getting someone elected than laborious policy explanations.[5] By percentage, few voters actually sit down and have a meaningful chat with a candidate seeking national office. Most voters depend on the portrayal of the candidate in the national media, especially television. Significantly, television is all about touching the heartstrings of its viewers and not their economic interests.[6] Television ads avoid detailed rational

[5] See Joe McGinness, *The Selling of The President 1968* (New York: Trident Press, 1969).
[6] See Neil Postman, *Amusing Ourselves to Death: Public Discourse in the Age of Show Business* (New York: Penguin Books, 1985).

explanations. Myth and ideals are what matter, which explains the strong emotional *feelings* party loyalists on both sides share.

But what are the ideals that Republicans and Democrats appeal to? In public discourse we use the terms "conservative" and "liberal" to distinguish between the ideals of Republicans and Democrats. Most Americans probably have a gut feeling for what a liberal or conservative is, and there is undoubtedly some consistency as to what these terms mean. In general, it is believed that liberals favor choice regarding abortion, social programs, lower defense spending, higher taxes, environmental protection, gun control, affirmative action for minority groups, workers, the poor, diversity, and big government. Liberals are against prayer in schools, hate speech, gender and sexual discrimination, and tax breaks for the wealthy. Conservatives, on the other hand, are considered to oppose abortion, social programs, higher taxes, environmentalism, gun control, affirmative action, diversity, and big government. Conservatives favor more defense spending, prayer and the Pledge of Allegiance in schools, business, lower taxes, English as the national language, strong crime laws and the war on drugs. Nevertheless, in spite of the fact that such a list comes easy, this distinction between conservatives and liberals is superficial; underlying these superficial differences is a set of commonly shared and deeply felt political ideals that are complex, confusing, and even contradictory.

Moreover, these ideals are primarily experienced as feelings, unquestioned beliefs as opposed to demonstrable facts. As such, they are quite vulnerable to any serious rational scrutiny. This helps explain why so much seems at stake to those deeply involved in partisan politics. Political ideals resemble religious ideals: even though they cannot be proven, they form the core of one's worldview. In this sense, political ideals are mythical. They provide meaning and value without being subjected to critical analysis.

The American Classic Liberal Heritage

Though the Constitution is the standard that American government in practice is held to, the document that best captures many of America's political ideals is Thomas Jefferson's Declaration of Independence, and this document is rooted in the writings of the English philosopher John Locke.[7] Political philosophers refer to Locke's writings as classic *liberal* theory, a definition that confuses most Americans today, who tend to view a liberal as someone who believes in the list mentioned above. However, the doctrine espoused by Locke and eventually by Jefferson is liberal in a historical sense. It aspired to overthrow the then conservative ideals that stood for monarchy, service to the crown, and a rigid class structure. Furthermore it is liberal in the philosophical sense that it aspired to liberate individuals both politically and economically. This classic *liberal* heritage ultimately underlies the basic beliefs of both Republicans and Democrats, or of both conservatives and liberals in America today. It could be argued that to some extent conservatives are trying to conserve essential classic *liberal* ideals where liberals are still attempting to realize them. Both groups share a classic *liberal* core.

Classic *liberalism* provides a unique, complex and contradictory perspective on the world. It starts with the fundamental assumption of individual freedoms bestowed by God, and limits government's primary role to the preservation of those freedoms.

Liberalism's Mythical Appeal

As mentioned above, the Declaration of Independence is the key document for understanding the basic beliefs of American political culture. It is

---

[7] Though I suggest that many of Jefferson's writings are founded on the writings of Locke, it would be simplistic to conclude that Locke is the personal founder of classic liberal theory. Locke is a product of his time and his writings reflect the ideas that were beginning to take hold during his day. See John Locke, *The Second Treatise on Government.*

rooted in the classic *liberal* concepts of self-evident truths, natural law, and the unalienable rights of individuals bestowed by God. In Jefferson's time, the then *liberal* dogma of Locke and others was shaping political thought throughout the western world.[8] Significantly, *liberalism* was initially a revolutionary dogma—serving primarily as a critique of the dominant views of divine right monarchy, and an emphasis on social obligation. As an answer to divine rights and monarchy, it was perhaps imperative for *liberalism* to seek legitimization by its appeal to God. But for whatever reason, the appeal makes *liberalism* a moral faith based on a firm belief in an understanding of God's will. This same moral conviction underlies the Declaration of Independence. With a religious claim to self-evident truths, the Declaration cries out for a holy war—calling upon men to rise up and accept the responsibility given them by their "Creator."

These God-given truths, accepted as unquestioned doctrine, underlie everything else in American political culture. They are held like any other religious faith. Their self-evidence puts them beyond question and gives them a mythical quality.[9] They have value particularly because they cannot be subjected to empirical testing and observation. One can only feel with unwavering confidence that they are self-evident.

Today's liberals and conservatives are equally grounded in this doctrine. The *moral* certitude liberals experience regarding a woman's right to choose is as faith-based as the conservatives' unwillingness to entertain doubts over the businessman's right to self-governance. For American political culture, political ideology is a religion.[10]

---

[8] See Bernard Bailyn, *The Ideological Origins of the American Revolution* (Cambridge: Harvard University Press, 1967).

[9] Daniel Boorstin refers to the American tendency to assume its core beliefs are true as "givenness," and argues that this is the "genius of American politics." See Boorstin, *The Genius of American Politics* (Chicago: The University of Chicago Press, 1953).

[10] For a good discussion of American political evangelism, see Louis Hartz, *The Liberal Tradition in America* (New York: Harcourt Brace & World, Incorporated, 1955).

Liberalism, Government's Role and the Myth of Natural Law

As a revolutionary dogma, *liberalism* was principally concerned with justifying the overthrow of what was perceived as an unjust regime. But serious *liberals* had to do more than simply justify revolution. They were also compelled to answer the perennial questions of politics. They had to explain the nature of social obligations and determine the legitimate exercise of power over others. By envisioning a natural state of humanity, consisting of autonomous individuals existing outside of society with God-given unalienable rights, *liberalism* made the answers to these questions self-evident as well.

Simply stated, *liberalism* answers the challenges of government by assuming them all away. Governance is conceived as being really quite easy, a matter of listening to common sense or a mythical natural law based on common sense. As Locke reasoned, the laws of nature teach all reasonable individuals that, just as they prefer being left alone to govern themselves, so too must they leave all others alone with regard to their lives, liberty and property. It is really that simple. Indeed Locke was convinced that there would be no need for government at all if everyone would just be reasonable and obey this natural law. It follows that government has one job: to insure that individuals remain free from intrusions by all violators of natural law.[11] Government must of course do this without becoming too intrusive itself, which ultimately makes governing much more difficult than it might initially sound. But nevertheless, *liberalism* assumes that all questions about governance can be resolved simply by listening to common sense. Government need not be complex at all if people will just be reasonable.

Though this summary of the *liberal* view of government is necessarily somewhat superficial, the fact remains that *liberalism* does view proper government simplistically. Absent is any notion that individual rights might possibly come into legitimate conflict that cannot be resolved by turning to

---

[11] John Locke, *Second Treatise on Government.*

natural law. If there is a conflict, *liberalism* can only assume that someone is not being reasonable in his or her pursuit of happiness. Witness for example the way the debate over abortion is framed in America today. Some cite common sense to argue that an adult woman should have power to make choices regarding her own body. From this perspective, government bureaucracies have no business meddling in such private affairs. The issue is that simple. There is no serious attempt to see that another individual's rights might be in direct conflict with the woman's right to choose. On the other hand, "Pro-life" advocates glibly refuse to admit that restricting a woman's right to choose an abortion is any restriction whatsoever. The woman is free to choose not to get pregnant, they argue, but her rights end there. In this simplistic way, they refuse to even entertain the question of a woman's right to regulate her own body, thus refusing to admit that in the case of abortion, two sets of individual rights might actually be in direct conflict. In short, both positions suffer from the classic *liberal* unwillingness to admit the possibility of legitimate conflicts between individual rights. Both focus on one side of the equation and assume that there can be no conflict between truly reasonable individuals. Moreover, both look to government to protect the individual rights they believe are self-evident.

To put it differently, classic *liberal* theory over-simplifies the challenge of social unity. *Liberalism* locates legitimate social cohesion in the rational self-interest of the individuals within that society. The only meaningful human interaction *liberalism* acknowledges is self-interested interaction. By assuming that the state of nature consists of autonomous free individuals (not groups), *liberalism* does not necessarily assume that humans are not social, but it does suggest that government's only responsibility is to preserve the individual's private interest, and that all relationships serve rationally calculated individual utility. In *The Wealth of Nations*, *liberal* free trade advocate Adam Smith openly argues that selfishness and nothing else holds legitimate society together and that to flourish, a free society needs nothing other than individuals motivated by pure self-interest. Smith argued that the butcher or baker's selfishness, not their benevolence, keeps them practicing their trade and providing their services to society. It follows, he reasoned, that government's primary responsibility is to keep these individuals free to pursue their self-interested endeavors. Social cohesion, he argued, forged by such selfishness, would be strong since it was based on individual interest and hence would naturally take care of itself. People help each other because they see it in their own personal interest to do so, and not because it is something they should do according to idealistic principles.

Smith had a point. Social cohesion based on individual interest is no doubt stronger than forced unity. Nevertheless, this does not make the *liberal* answer to the question of society and governance any less simplistic. Critics of *liberal* theory have questioned the legitimacy of the abstract theory of autonomous individuals. For starters, they note that no one exists as a completely autonomous individual enjoying the individual rights Locke envisioned. At the very least, critics charge, humans from birth depend on others for their survival, and one cannot help but wonder about *liberal* theory's willingness to reason this dependence away.[12] If, for example, humans naturally exist in a social setting with deep and necessary connections with one another, perhaps any thorough answer to the questions of governance must take this into consideration.

The Myth of Majority Rule

Faith in common sense, coupled with the belief that rational individuals can easily get along, results in the *liberal* view that governing requires no particular skills or wisdom. Any reasonably thinking adult can understand the basic principle of governance: all individuals should be left free to pursue happiness in their individual ways without infringing on the right of others to do

[12] In *The Public and its Problems*, for example, John Dewey, criticizes Locke's assumption that individuals are the basic unit in the state of nature and wonders why Locke did not consider free communities as fundamental. Anarchist philosophers also question this liberal assumption. For example, Peter Kropotkin's 1902 publication *Mutual Aid* argued it is human social nature best accounts for the tremendous success of homo sapiens.

the same. Nevertheless, because government must protect individuals from those who do not respect common sense, and must do so without violating common sense itself, the inevitable result is that governments simply cannot act without causing some individual to feel wronged. For example, governments cannot act without the means to act. Gaining the means requires raising revenue, which has historically meant some form of taxation. Yet many perceive taxation as an imposition on individual freedom and hence the violation of natural law. So how does one decide the legitimate means government can use to do its job? *Liberalism's* answer to this question is again predictably simplistic—common sense.

Though many Americans view government as a necessary evil[13], *liberalism* actually does grant government a positive role. Locke argued that it would be inconvenient for individuals to govern themselves, and he reasoned that it was therefore more beneficial for all individuals to let someone else do this in order to free the individual for personal pursuits. Knowing this, the reasonable individual would clearly consent to provide government with the means necessary to carry out its basic functions. Hence taxation does not necessarily violate natural law, provided that government takes no more than it needs to carry out these fundamental responsibilities.

Locke further argued that though individuals can listen to reason, most favor their shortsighted personal desires when in conflict with others and thereby tend to disregard natural law. An impartial judge must therefore settle disputes between partial individuals. Here *liberalism* puts its faith in the majority, believing that a people acting as a majority is more likely to create impartiality than single individuals acting on their own. Hence governments blessed by the majority are considered legitimate.

[13] See Garry Wills, *A Necessary Evil: A History of American Distrust of Government* (New York: Simon & Schuster, 1999).

This faith in the majority's impartiality is also overly simplistic and mythical to its very core. It is certainly not self-evident. For example, anyone ever caught up in the fanatical frenzy of fans at a sporting event knows it is quite possible for individuals to act even less rationally as members of a group than they might on their own. Indeed, as will be argued momentarily, fear of an irrational majority deeply concerned the framers of the Constitution. Nevertheless, the belief in the rational majority remains a key myth in *liberal* thinking.

For early *liberal* writers such as Locke, individuals unwilling to abide by majority rule were undoubtedly too partial to their own interests and hence irrational and outside of the laws of nature. Assuming that the only acceptable government enjoys majority support, *liberalism* further assumes that all rationally enlightened individuals will willingly submit to the majority's demands even though they might impinge on an individual's immediate self-interests. The alternatives are worse. In fact, *liberalism* suggests that individuals unwilling to consent to the majority will implicitly wish to subject the majority to their will. This is the essence of dictatorship. Forcing the majority to sacrifice its interests to the selfish demands of a single individual is the very thing Jefferson accused King George of in the Declaration of Independence.

Hence, *liberal* theory reasons, all individuals in a society should submit to majority consent, indeed anyone benefiting from government services tacitly consents to be governed. By implication, unreasonable dissenters are always welcome to leave or pay the penalty. This explains how a "freedom-loving" country can have slogans such as "America: Love it or Leave it," and why Americans submit so readily to the outcome of a hotly fought political contest even when on the losing side.[14] As long as the majority is perceived to prevail,

[14] The observant reader may see the 2000 presidential election as a challenge to this line of argument. In that election, the winner did not get the popular vote yet Americans still quickly fell in line, suggesting that a government does not necessarily have to have the support of the majority to be legitimate. This is a good observation. Why did Americans not see the Bush presidency as

liberal ideals teach that the result is rational and therefore right. Hence the myth that the majority is always right, although simplistic, helps to insure government stability and relatively peaceful changes in government despite the revolutionary nature of *liberal* theory. Nevertheless, as will be demonstrated in the next section, faith in the majority rule myth cannot entirely put to rest the question of government legitimacy.

The Right to Revolution Myth

Chief among the ideals reflected in Jefferson's Declaration is the right, and even moral *obligation*, to revolt from an illegitimate government. Taking his cue from Locke, Jefferson reasoned that when government consistently fails to live up to its primary responsibility of insuring individual liberties, it is no longer legitimate. According to *liberal* theory, though rational individuals would naturally give up their powers of self-governance to a government committed to preserving individual rights, individuals can never truly give up the responsibility of self-governance. All individuals have a moral obligation to insure that their rights are preserved. Because, as Locke reasoned, individuals received their rights from God, they were directly answerable to God and not government. By the same logic, Jefferson claimed that individuals were "endowed by their Creator with certain unalienable Rights" and that "whenever any Form of Government becomes destructive of these ends, it is the Right of the People to alter or to abolish it, and to institute new Government."

Though Locke took seriously the responsibility to abolish illegitimate government it has proven rather problematic. Locke believed that the majority, not just single individuals, needed to feel that government was violating individual liberties. Individuals tend to be too partial to their own particular

nothing short of the essence of dictatorship? Indeed, some critics did. Nevertheless, *liberal* myths only tell part of the story and as will be discussed in Chapter Three, American *liberalism* is tempered by republican myths similar to those of Plato where wise leaders are sometimes considered necessary to save the majority from itself.

interests. Significantly, Jefferson provides a long laundry list of abuses to justify the abolition of George the Third's rule over the colonists. Nevertheless, majorities consist of individuals, and implied in the right to revolt, is the concept that individual's speak up and act decisively when government abuses its power.

This obviously contradicts the notion of tacit consent and majority rule. What if the majority acts against the laws of nature? As mentioned above, by the time of Thomas Jefferson, many considered majorities capable of tyrannical actions. Surely a person who tacitly consents to being governed by an illegitimate government is as guilty of tyranny as those acting in an official capacity. Indeed, those British citizens living in the American colonies who opposed the dissolution of British rule appear as unpatriotic traitors in American mythology while those individuals willing to risk all in violation of government tyranny are celebrated as heroes.

To sum up, in American political mythology individuals have the *moral* obligation to both zealously support legitimate government and to zealously revolt against illegitimate government, and are expected to know which is which. But how does one know when to support and when to revolt? Simple! It is self-evident to all individuals who will just listen to reason. Moreover, since the answer, rooted in moral natural law, is considered so easy, it is no wonder that the debate between active Republicans and Democrats creates such intense feelings. Because both parties share the classic *liberal* faith that moral truth is self-evident to any reasonably thinking individual, they cannot attribute their differences to anything short of self-deception or shortsighted selfishness. Republicans and Democrats alike believe the other party wants to use government for illegitimate and hence immoral ends. Since *liberal* myth imposes moral obligation to resist tyrannical government, this perception cannot be dismissed lightly.

The Myth of Representation

While the responsibility to revolt seriously complicates the majority rule myth, the complexity does not end there. Jefferson's Declaration actually puts its faith in the "People" with a capital P. And this idea has a significantly different connotation than Locke's majority rule ideal. Though Jefferson himself was relatively committed to democratic principles, many of Jefferson's time had little faith in the people's ability to know what was best for them. This skepticism toward the majority would eventually be institutionalized in key provisions adopted at the Constitutional Convention. For example, the decision to use the Electoral College to select the president of the United States reduced the majority's direct impact to fill that most important office. Jefferson's use of "People" actually implies the belief that a rational, enlightened will of the people may exist in opposition to the vocal majority of people. President Lincoln, in his first inaugural address, used this concept and consistently saw himself as representing the enlightened will of the people, whether they knew it or not. More recently, President Richard Nixon coined the phrase "Silent Majority" to refer to the will of people he saw himself representing and certain members of the right wing of the Republican Party have seen themselves as representing the "Moral Majority."

Significantly, the Declaration's signers are referred to as "Representatives" of "the good People" of the colonies. The preamble to the Constitution states "We the People of the United States" even though no majority of U.S. citizens in 1789 wrote and ratified that document, but rather individuals who saw themselves as representatives of the People of the United States, or the people with the proper understanding of certain political ideals. This is not to suggest that representation is necessarily undemocratic. But it does suggest a paternalistic element in American political mythology, a significant departure from the theory that majority consent gives government its legitimacy.

Since the time of the founders, it could be argued that America has consistently moved further and further away from accepting this type of paternalism and more toward actual majority rule. One could cite greater voting rights, and a flood of referendums on the ballots of many states. Nevertheless, the fact still remains that some paternalism is not only tolerated, but actually extolled, by many Americans. For example, the first President Bush enjoyed high approval ratings, despite his aggressive press censorship during the Persian Gulf War. His son enjoyed a similar popularity with similarly paternalistic policies meant to strengthen homeland security. It is by no means radical in America today to suggest that government leaders know best. In fact, as we saw following the terrorist attacks of 9/11, at times it can be considered downright unpatriotic to even question the president.

This belief in paternalistic representatives departs significantly from the classic *liberal* ideal that underlies much of American political culture and will be examined in greater depth in Chapter Three. The ideal of representation also has a less paternalistic, more majoritarian element. The practice of selecting representatives by majority vote through elections responds primarily to the ideal of majority rule and is consistent with the notion that legitimate government carries out the will of the majority. In this sense, representatives are seen as representing the voice of the people. It could be argued that the Constitution envisions Congress as the government institution tied most directly to the public, and for that reason grants it the responsibility for making laws that reflect the will of the people. Nor has this representative ideal disappeared with the acceptance of a more activist president. Indeed, strong presidents claim to have the legitimacy to set national agendas because they are the only officials elected by the American public at large. When presidential approval ratings lag, Congress is most assertive.[15]

---

[15] Cronin, T. "Resurgent Congress and the Imperial Presidency," Political Science Quarterly, 95 (Summer, 1980): 209-37.

Finally, the idea of representation serves a third ideal in American political culture that is also consistent with classic *liberal* theory. The primary, legally supported means of raising the revenue necessary to run a political campaign in America is still private contributions, which by definition originate in private, special interests. The legitimacy of this method of funding public elections depends on the *liberal* ideal of individual rights. Representatives are expected to represent not only the majority interests of their constituencies, but also the individual interests of each of their constituents, or at least of all those constituents who make direct contact with them. Moreover, members of Congress in both houses are expected to provide special services for individuals directly, and much of their time and energy, as well as their staff's time and resources, are spent on individual requests. In short, federal tax dollars pay the salaries of hundreds of people who spend much of their time promoting private, individual agendas, suggesting that the ideal of representation in American politics significantly answers to the ideal of *liberal* individualism and its demand that government be used to promote individual self-interests.

In sum, the ideal of representation in American political mythology actually serves three significantly different, even contradictory ideals: paternalism, majoritarianism, and individualism. The paternalistic ideal, inconsistent with the *liberal* emphasis on individual initiative and majority will, is examined in further detail in Chapter Three along with other deviations from *liberalism*. What is significant for this chapter is that all three ideals exist simultaneously and make contradictory demands. And as if this were not enough, the conflicting demands on government by American political culture become even more complex and paradoxical with the addition of the Bill of Rights.

The Logic of the Bill of Rights

Though we regard the Bill of Rights as a necessary component of American democracy, it actually implies deep skepticism about the democratic process and representative government, changing the meaning of democracy radically. In one sense, the Bill of Rights relies neither on a majority nor on paternalistic representatives to determine what is best for the group. Instead it relies on the rule of law, that is, a government of law and not of people. In fact, though the Constitution itself could be viewed primarily as a document that provides the rules for the democratic process, the concept of relying on rules is, in a certain sense, undemocratic. If the people are governed by rules, then the rules and not the people are sovereign.

Nevertheless, including the Bill of Rights in the American Constitution is consistent with classic *liberal* belief in natural law. Indeed to Americans, the Constitution, in some respects, actually represents natural law. It is viewed as a sacred document, "handed down" (like an heirloom pocket watch) by wise "founding fathers" (as opposed to "first politicians,") to protect us from short sighted and self-interested politicians.[16] The Bill of Rights starts with the assumption that individuals have rights that exist prior to government and must therefore be preserved first and foremost.

On the other hand, in one particular way the logic of the Bill of Rights runs contrary to that of early *liberal* writers. Locke believed a government acting with the consent of the majority would be the most legitimate government, because he believed that majority opinion was more likely to harmonize with natural law than the opinions of individuals, inevitably partial to their own desires. The Bill of Rights could thus be viewed as displaying a clear distrust of the majority, as it suggests that certain individual rights must be maintained regardless of majority opinion.

In short, the Bill of Rights arguably uses *liberal* faith in the rule of natural law to undermine *liberal* faith in majority rule, a problem compounded by the Ninth Amendment, which states that individual rights are not limited to those

---

[16] In his book *A Parliament of Whores*, P.J. O'Rourke refers to the founding fathers as the "original dads." The fact that O'Rourke's terminology seems irreverent indicates the aura of sanctity with which American political mythology endows the early politicians.

explicitly stated in the Constitution. The Ninth Amendment implies that an exhaustive list of individual liberties could not be anticipated and its insertion makes it virtually impossible for government to act without appearing to violate someone's rights. By the logic of the Bill of Rights a majoritarian government cannot be the impartial body that settles disputes between partial individuals.

However, in other ways, the Bill of Rights does not undermine the belief in the majority's ability to determine natural law at all. If the people write the law, then the people and not the law are sovereign. And in fact, a greater body of people than those attending the Constitutional Convention demanded that the Bill of Rights be included in the Constitution. Furthermore, the Constitution can be amended by a very large majority of people, suggesting an ultimate faith in the majority. In this way, the existence of the Constitution with its Bill of Rights is in direct harmony with the myth that a majority is more likely to be in tune with natural law than the shortsighted individual. By considering the Constitution preeminent, Americans reveal their distrust of representatives and the ordinary legislative process, and their great faith in the super majority it takes to pass Constitutional Amendments.[17]

Significantly, both ideals are present in American political mythology. The Constitution both represents a natural law binding on majorities and individuals alike, while allowing amendment by a super majority—suggesting that ultimately Americans put their faith in the wisdom of the majority.

The Myth of Property Rights

As American commitment to capitalism suggests, property rights are also fundamental to American political culture. Nevertheless, it would be misleading to simply state that Americans respect private property, and move on. In fact, in some ways property rights receive very little respect in America. For example,

---

[17] As will be discussed in Chapter Four, Bruce Ackerman makes this assumption—his primary reason for arguing that the Supreme Court acts democratically when it overturns an act of Congress not in harmony with the people's will as reflected in the Constitution.

individuals may not grow marijuana on private property, or raise hogs in the middle of an urban area. Private businesses are not completely free to determine whom to hire and cannot choose to withhold services based on race. Moreover, it is legal for government to take private property in the way of taxes, and redistribute private property by giving welfare to the poor and large subsidies to many business enterprises. In short, private property rights are not absolutes in America. What ideal, then, do Americans rely on to distinguish proper and improper government activity with regard to property rights?

Much actual policy-making with regard to property rights arguably has more to do with vested interests and positions of power than any ideals or guiding principles. To be sure, special-interest lobbying determines the direction of government spending. Furthermore, the fact that a senior member of the U.S. Senate represents a state that grows a lot of tobacco cannot be overlooked in trying to determine why tobacco farming is legal and even subsidized in America while marijuana farming is not. Nevertheless, as argued above, it would be myopic to view politics as solely the purview of special interests, and the point of this essay is to understand the ideals or myths that legitimize policy choices for the majority of American voters. After all, politicians seeking national office do their best to distance themselves from special interests during the campaign and try to at least appear to run on principles. What are these principles? What ideal justifies taxing the middle class and giving aid to the poor and even greater aid to large businesses and corporations?

Like others, this ideal is also rooted in the *liberal* logic of Locke's *Second Treatise on Government*. Recall that Locke's major objective in writing the *Second Treatise* was to justify the overthrow of a system where the vast majority of individuals owned no land and were subject to the whims of those few large landholders that owned it all. Significantly, Locke viewed property rights as key to all individual liberty. As long as individuals are dependent on others for their physical needs, Locke reasoned, they are not really free at all. This too is a significant element of American mythology. Though Americans no longer believe that individuals must actually own land to be free, they do believe that to be free one must at least be able to choose one's employer and therefore avoid dependence on any one particular boss. In other words, property rights in America serve loftier purposes than individual greed. Property rights are considered necessary for political freedom, and to question property rights is to aim at the heart of the American ideal of freedom. For this reason, obligatory taxation to promote government programs is inherently suspect and must ultimately be justified in the name of insuring property rights. Questions concerning welfare, the minimum wage, and the availability of high-paying jobs are also critical. If one is not truly economically free, the ideal of America being the land of the free is suspect.

Locke began his treatise on property with what he considered the big question: since God had originally given all humans (Locke actually used the word "men") joint ownership of the entire world, how could any individual legitimately lay claim to private ownership of anything? For today's political philosopher, this is obviously a question loaded with dubious assumptions. Before answering it, we might note another important element in American mythology.

Though all ideals are mythical insofar as they cannot be empirically proven the way a budding scientist might prove the temperature at which water freezes, it is nevertheless at least theoretically possible to debate the merits of one ideal over another. But the *liberal* political mythology does not even allow this kind of debate. This too is significant. When a society's ideals forbid questions about the value of its first principles, an underlying sense of vulnerability is inevitable.[18] This insecurity is often overcome through zealous belief.[19] Such belief is not inherently politically weak. In fact, unquestioned faith can quite

[18] See John Stuart Mill, *On Liberty*.
[19] See Alasdair MacIntyre, *After Virtue*, chapters 1-3.

effectively unite a group of individuals with an intensity often found in American political culture. Though some do question American ideals (as is evidenced by this manuscript,) challenges to the fundamental mythology have thus far failed to significantly affect mainstream American politics. In an American election campaign, the label "socialist" or even "environmentalist," for example, has moral tones analogous to the label "heretic" in religious circles. There is no quicker way to end debate. (Al Gore understood this as he attempted to distance himself from the "E" word in the 2000 presidential race.)

Now back to Locke's big question: if God had originally given all humans joint ownership of the entire world, how could any person legitimately lay claim to individual ownership of anything? One of his purposes in asking this question was to legitimize the breaking up of large estates. In doing so, however, he could not question the principle of private ownership per se, as he viewed private ownership imperative for liberty. In short, Locke needed to determine the just limits of private property in order to allow private property rights for all. This is an important point. The logic that underlies the American concept of property rights demands a limit to individual property rights. Only with this in mind, can we really understand the meaning of property rights in American political culture.

Just as no economically dependent individual is truly free, Locke reasoned, so long as everyone owns everything jointly, no one can really be economically independent. In order even to eat, for example, individuals must consume something that belongs to everyone else, where everyone owns everything. How then, can anyone claim a right to anything? Locke answers by positing first that, at the very least, individuals originally have the right to private ownership of themselves and their labor.[20] From this, Locke deduced that if a person were to mix his or her labor with that which is jointly owned by all, that object becomes his or hers and no one else's, provided that there is as much left

[20] For Karl Marx, the conception of ownership in self has serious ramifications that will not be explored in this essay. This topic is carefully analyzed in Marx's early writings, particularly the *Economic and Philosophic Manuscripts of 1844*.

over in common for everyone else.[21] For example, so long as there is enough good water left for all others, the man who has dipped his cup into a river to drink has not really taken anything from the rest of the group, and that which is in his cup clearly belongs to him and no one else.

Today, as the world's resources look increasingly finite, perhaps it could be argued that Locke committed a terrible oversight with this assumption. Could he not foresee the exponential growth rate of human kind to the point that there would be no good land left to develop for the benefit of all? What then? But Locke did foresee this, and he addressed it in a way that modern American political mythology has also adopted. As long as there is plenty of good land left for others, Locke reasoned, not only is the man who grows wheat on a formerly uncultivated piece of land not a thief, he has actually done humanity a great service by increasing the amount of food available for all. And though there may be very little if any actual land left for individuals needing a fresh start, American political culture still uses this logic to distinguish legitimate from illegitimate private property. Legitimate private industry is highly valued in America because it is viewed as increasing the opportunities for all. Good industry creates job opportunities, justifying tax breaks and government subsidies. Moreover, good industry benefits everyone by providing new investment opportunities. Bill Gates, for example, was not born the wealthiest man in the world. He made his fortune by taking advantage of the many opportunities created by the great private industry that preceded him. Furthermore, he is allowed to pursue his wealth only as long as he is viewed as helping many others in their pursuit of wealth as well. To the degree that Gates is perceived as engaging in practices that lead to monopoly control akin to that of Locke's landlords, his industry rouses suspicion.

Similarly, bad industry is viewed as industry that destroys the environment in unacceptable ways. Hydroelectric dams are coming under increasing attack primarily because they are seen as damaging the environment irreparably. In

---

[21] See Locke's *Second Treatise* and the chapter titled *Of Property*.

short, Locke's imperative that there be limits to individual property rights very much informs the way even conservation groups and environmentalists frame political questions. National parks and recreation areas are preserved precisely because American political mythology demands that there be limits to individual industry. God gave ownership of the world to all humans jointly, and an individual may only claim private property as long as there is enough left for everyone else to enjoy. [22]

Indeed, much of the political debate over property rights in America revolves around the question of the possibility of ever expanding opportunities. Once one begins with the assumption of God-given rights to life, liberty, and property for *all* individuals, it is impossible to justify the property rights of any single individual without considering the impact of those rights on others. As long as Americans want to believe that all individuals have property rights, they must also believe in endless opportunity. If once such opportunities are perceived as finite, many individual liberties can legitimately be regulated. Just as Locke condemned the system a great landholdings because it limited individual liberty for the vast majority of individuals, so too would American liberties be illegitimate once opportunities were perceived as limited. Americans seem to intuitively sense this—hence their fascination with a new frontier. Indeed perhaps much of the debate Westerners have with their Eastern cousins over national parks and wildlife preserves has to do with differing perceptions of how much frontier is still available to all. It is also no accident that ever since the unpopular Jimmy Carter told Americans the time had come to turn thermostats down in the name of energy conservation, American presidents have all gone back to singing the song of endless opportunity.

---

[22] Indeed, the many national parks and wildlife preserves suggests that in America there is a certain commitment to preserving nature that at times prevails even when in direct conflict with the economic interests of many individual. Leo Marx thoroughly explores the full dichotomy in American political culture regarding nature in the *Machine in the Garden*.

To sum up, property rights are an integral piece of American political mythology consisting of five significant elements. It does not matter whether these beliefs are true. The point is that each makes its presence felt in American political debate. First, the mythology views property rights as key to any meaningful concept of liberty. The individual who has no choice but to work for another cannot really be free. Second, the concept of property rights is based on an unexamined faith in private ownership as a divine principle, a self-evident truth not open for debate. Third, property rights, though absolutely necessary to individual freedom, are not absolutes, the property rights of one individual can exist only in conjunction with the property rights of all individuals. Fourth, the property rights of every individual ultimately depend on the possibility of endless opportunity. And finally, individual initiative and industry makes it all possible, granting the right to property in the first place, and making it possible to keep scarcity at bay.

These five factors must each be reckoned with in all questions concerning property rights in American politics. Any politician hoping to get elected must accept the right to private property as an absolute moral truth, regardless of party affiliation. Similarly, no serious candidate can reject the principle of equal opportunity. If all the good opportunities are gone, no single individual has an absolute right to property any more than the landlords in Locke's day, and all successful candidates acknowledge that government must protect the property interests of all by insuring opportunity. On the other hand, when there is plenty of opportunity, government redistribution of wealth through progressive tax policies and welfare becomes unquestionably illegitimate. Hence the debate between Republicans and Democrats often revolves around how best to insure opportunity. Significantly, no party can question the possibility for endless opportunity; to do so would jeopardize the myth of property rights altogether. Furthermore, people in both parties feel morally obliged to answer these questions correctly, which helps explain the passion displayed in both camps even though both agree on the principle ideals. Finally, in spite of the many cries to limit government interference, people in both parties ultimately feel that government must play an important role in answering the questions of property, as individuals themselves cannot be relied on to act fairly and impartially. But, as discussed above, the logic of the Bill of Rights suggests that a government elected by the majority cannot always be trusted to be impartial in preserving inherent individual property rights. All government action is highly suspect.

Conclusion

American political mythology is rich with conflicting ideals deeply felt and imbued with religious moral certitude. Implicit is the faith that the challenges of government are inherently simple; that an objective truth exists that absolutely cannot be open to question; that this truth is in harmony with Deity; that the nature of this truth is self-evident to all who are really honest and upright; that the unalienable individual rights of all citizens can coincide so long as everyone is committed to obeying nature's law; and that good citizens should and will feel obligated to act decisively when government disobeys the self-evident natural law.

These fundamental ideals work under the surface in American political discourse today. Due to their strong moral appeal, people involved in politics often feel a deep and acute sense of urgency to get the right people in office. Similarly, people often feel deeply betrayed by public officials and consider folks in office not just wrong but actually evil. No wonder Republicans and Democrats fear each other's dominance. Both camps share fundamental assumptions about the truths they believe and the crucial conviction that opposing views must be morally flawed. To the sincere American patriot, every political battle is in a sense a holy war.

The moral appeal of these ideals explains the emotional passion of those involved in political races in spite of the fact that policy differences between the two major parties are seldom that radical. But it is also significant that the ideals themselves are so contradictory that no lasting resolution will ever be possible.

The faith in majority rule is simultaneously contradicted by a deeply held fear of the majority. The belief in the majority leads Americans to cry out with great passion "LOVE IT OR LEAVE IT," yet some of their most heroic stories are of patriotic individuals who neither loved it nor left it, but defied it.

The Constitution is viewed as sacred, natural law, handed down by wise founding fathers to check untoward majority zeal. Yet Americans contradict this belief by passionately rallying the majority behind calls to amend the Constitution when it fails to provide them with what they expect and want.

Americans look to paternalistic representatives to save them from themselves, yet at the same time charge their representatives to be responsive to the will of the majority, all while expecting them personally and selectively to aide those individuals frustrated by the majority's rules.

Finally, individual property rights are viewed as sacred, outside of the public realm, and absolutely fundamental to individual liberty. Yet this belief ultimately subjects all property rights to public scrutiny and possible regulation as the myth that all have a right to economic freedom is dependent on the possibility of non-interference and endless opportunity. In practice, the result has been tremendous government involvement in economic matters, as individual initiative and industry are only valued insofar as they appear to at least not interfere with the opportunities of others and at most create new opportunities for economic growth.

It would be nearly impossible to prioritize these ideals in terms of their importance to American political culture. Nor are any of them exclusively the purview of Democrats or Republicans. Americans in the political mainstream in both parties believe them all, passionately and simultaneously.

Most importantly, it should not be concluded, as does H. Mark Roelofs in *The Poverty of American Politics*, that the existence of these contradicting

American ideals is a weakness.[23] In fact, just the opposite is true. This is the very *richness* of American politics. American political mythology is most interesting and valuable precisely because it has so many contradictions. Indeed, the very genius of American politics (to use a phrase coined by Daniel Boorstin[24]) is that its contradicting ideals work always to keep any single political position somewhat off balance, checking political activity regardless of which party is in power. For example, when Republicans argue for greater government interference in the name of public safety and crime control, Democrats can look to the ideal of individual liberty and demand that excessive government interference be tempered. Or when Democrats, moved by the ideal of property rights, seek greater government interference in terms of welfare, Republicans use elements of the same ideal to demand that excessive government involvement be questioned. When government leaders demand obedience to preserve liberty, critics demand civil disobedience for the same reason. When President Bush wanted to tap oil reserves in Alaska, he felt compelled to argue that the impact on the environment would be limited. This is the strength of American political mythology. It is much more difficult for a government to act in a totalitarian and despotic way when its very legitimacy is based on ideals that pull it in different and conflicting directions. Perhaps meaningful liberty depends on contradictory ideals.

The more important question is how do we answer to the contradictions inherent in American political mythology without destroying them. How can America insure that the contradictions remain healthy and relevant? How do Americans insure that their rich *liberal* heritage continues to make its conflicting demands on government real and meaningful?

Ultimately, responsibility for preserving American political mythology falls on the American people; no single government institution can by itself insure that this happens. Nevertheless, to the extent that government institutions can

---

[23] H. Mark Roelofs, *The Poverty of American Politics: A Theoretical Interpretation* (Philadelphia: Temple University Press, 1992).
[24] See Boorstin, *The Genius of American Politics*.

play a role, the Supreme Court of the United States is key. In fact, as Chapter Five argues, preserving American political ideals is the Court's *essential* role. However, before this argument can be made, the broader question of how American political mythology understands the challenges of controlling government must be understood. This is the focus of the next chapter.

e pluribus unum

Chapter Two
American Mythology and Controlling Government

At this point, a brief word clarifying the phrase "American political culture" or "mythology" is in order. Arguably, no single American political culture or mythology exists, but rather a diverse society clearly displaying numerous racial, class, and ethnic differences. Moreover, significant differences characterize political cultures in different regions of the nation, making it deceptive to suggest that all Americans share the same political culture. Nevertheless, mainstream American voters do share a common set of ideals at the national level, ideals to which all successful presidential candidates appeal. Given our national media, presidential hopefuls must be careful about focusing too much on any particular regional ideal or mythology. Successful candidates speak to the lofty ideals and myths that span the nation and give meaning to our Fourth of July parades and other patriotic rallies. In fact, it may be these ideals, more than anything else, that unite America as a nation. As Tocqueville observed in the early 19th century, a large nation has significant economic and regional differences that seriously threaten to divide it—making a nation's myths all the more important as a unifying element.[25]

In practice, mythical ideals often remain just that, mythical ideals. Though they color our political debate and shape our expectations and notions of legitimacy, there are always hard economic interests at work as well. Perhaps this is why former Speaker of the House Tip O'Neil was known to say: "all politics is local." In spite of all the ideals, O'Neil recognized that real interests must be

[25] Alexis de Tocqueville, *Democracy in America*, Vol. I.

served. Yet this does not negate the role of mythical ideals in shaping policy. Political action must be justified morally as well as practically, making mythical ideals central to every political situation. E. H. Carr referred to this struggle between ideals and interests as "the stuff of politics" and viewed its presence as ubiquitous:

> There is no greater barrier to clear political thinking than failure to distinguish between ideals, which are utopia, and institutions, which are reality.... The ideal, once it is embodied in an institution, ceases to be an ideal and becomes the expression of a selfish interest.... This constant interaction of irreconcilable forces is the stuff of politics. Every political situation contains mutually incompatible elements of utopia and reality of morality and power.[26]

In Chapter One, we examined how the assumption that all are endowed with individual liberties creates in American political discourse irresolvable, yet rich and vital, contradicting ideals. It was also suggested that the Supreme Court has an important role in preserving these ideals. In this chapter, we examine how the basic assumption of individual rights shapes American expectations for actual *government institutions*, resulting in similar contradictions that prove to be essential to American liberty. Once again, I will propose that the Supreme Court has a vital role in preserving these contradictions as well.

Liberal Theory and Government Legitimacy

Liberal theory's first challenge is to legitimize government. Since *liberalism* assumes that individuals have a God-given right to freedom, it naturally asks why anyone should be obliged to obey government at all. As discussed in Chapter One, Locke answered by arguing that it would be terribly inconvenient if individuals were required to protect their own rights from all who might trespass against them, and that any truly enlightened individual would

---

[26] Edward Hallett Carr, *The Twenty Years' Crisis 1919-1939: An Introduction to the Study of International Relations* (London: MacMillan and Co. LTD, New York: St. Martin's Press, 1962), p. 93.

willingly submit to a government committed to preserving individual liberty. In other words, Locke reasoned, the best chance to fully enjoy individual liberty exists only when an established government established aids in securing those liberties. Nevertheless, in stating that individuals have rights prior to government, Locke meant primarily to establish that governments could be illegitimate when committed to preserving individual liberties. This is clearly the logic at work in the Declaration of Independence. Jefferson did not state that government as such is illegitimate; he argued only that the King of England was illegitimately violating the God given rights of the colonists.

As was also discussed in Chapter One, Locke's claim that all humans have a natural right to freedom depends on all respecting the freedom of others, which suggests that in *liberal* thought freedom is by definition limited. Locke argued that reason itself teaches that all should respect the natural rights of others, yet government is necessary because individuals do not always listen to reason. It follows that the primary challenge of governance is to *control* unreasonable individuals. In short, *liberal* theory assumes a society composed of autonomous individuals, each having a God-given right to pursue personal self-interest, yet each also prone to irrationality hence requiring restraint. Note that government is not conceived as having the positive or proactive responsibility of helping individuals become more reasonable, only of controlling unreasonable individuals. This too was a departure from earlier views of government. For centuries political philosophers and practitioners considered government's primary purpose as developing virtuous and upright citizens.[27] *Liberal* theory completely ignores this question and in fact leaves the door open for some to argue that a person's virtue is not the business of government whatsoever. The full significance of this tenet must be examined elsewhere. For now, note that *liberal* theory limits the purpose of government to controlling or containing

---

[27] See Plato's *The Republic* or Aristotle's *Politics* for example. Both Plato and Aristotle viewed government as having a public responsibility to aid in the development of virtue in its citizenry.

unacceptable behavior. This view was clearly uppermost in the mind of Madison or Hamilton (which of the two is still uncertain) in the following argument for adopting the Constitution. Note how the question posed is primarily one of control:

> If men were angels, no government would be necessary. If angels were to govern men, neither external nor internal controls on government would be necessary. In framing a government which is to be administered by men over men, the great difficulty lies in this: you must first enable the government to control the governed; and in the next place oblige it to control itself. (*Federalist Papers No. 51*)

Though Americans are consistently disenchanted with the blatant self-serving attitudes of the people they continue to put in office, significantly, the thinking in the above quote virtually *expects* government officials to use power for their own ends. Rather than looking for methods to insure that only unselfish individuals obtain government positions, *liberal* theory assumes that no such individual exists—men are not angels. In other words, *liberal* mythology rules out the possibility of upright politicians, and the important question becomes how to limit the actions of the inevitably self-seeking governors.

Some might argue that the *Federalist* argument is just realistic, that self-seeking individuals inevitably do end up in power and it is best to assume the worst. This may be so, but more importantly the very *ideal* America is founded on assumes untrustworthy government officials, so that Americans are *expected* simultaneously to distrust and rely on government leaders. But perhaps even more significant, if not astounding, is that *liberal* mythology not only expects men not to be angels, it actually celebrates their selfishness. *Liberal* theorist Adam Smith made a virtue out of the selfishness of the butcher and the baker, arguing that it was their individual selfishness and not their altruism that ultimately led to the greater wealth of the entire nation. Moreover, *liberal* thinkers viewed selfishness as constant, making it all the more reliable when pursuing the national good.[28] Believing that men are not angels, *liberalism* not only allows for, but celebrates self-serving politicians. No wonder Americans tolerate the spending of personal fortunes to get themselves and others elected. According to *liberal* logic, the most selfish individuals are the most publicly beneficial of all!

This element of American political culture has significant implications. One cannot help but wonder about a philosophy which openly encourages individuals to seek government positions in order to serve themselves. Not that the Founders abandoned the ideal of self-sacrificing virtue entirely. In fact, as will be discussed in Chapter Three, the *Federalist Papers* refers frequently to the importance of virtuous office holders and the Founders attempted to build in a process that would enhance and increase the chances that this would be the case. Nevertheless, as Tocqueville noted when he visited America, those most blinded by personal ambition often seek higher office. By making selfishness a virtue, Americans make it much more difficult to find self-sacrificing leaders. How do you tell the self-aggrandizer, with liberal theory behind him, to suddenly forego selfishness upon taking public office? But this is a question outside the scope of this paper. The question for now is the question of controlling the many individuals *liberalism* assumes will be in public office.

Because *liberal* mythology anticipates that when left completely free, the powerful seriously threaten the freedom of all others, the challenge is at once to allow individuals in government to freely pursue their own self-interest and to keep their pursuits within acceptable bounds.

As stated above, Locke's, and subsequently Jefferson's, claim that all individuals were endowed with God-given rights assumes that reason teaches us to respect the individual rights of others. And yet *liberal* theory also assumes that

---

[28] In *The Passions and The interests: Political Arguments for Capitalism Before Its Triumph*, Albert O. Hirschman provides a fascinating account of how *liberal* theorists came to view economic interests as capable of taming other passions. Moreover, such theorists viewed economic interests as constant and reliable making it possible to make the study of politics more scientific. In this way, *liberal* theory tends to over simplify politics by assuming it is only economic interests that really matter.

individuals are not inclined to listen to reason when their own interests are at stake, making it necessary for an impartial outside body to step in, judge, and regulate. Similarly, the Constitution's Framers attempted to insure legitimate government by creating a structure which denied any government official the final power to judge his or her own situation, in which universal reason could prevail, and in which some control could be enforced. Specifically, they attempted to do this by relying on four basic mechanisms: majority rule, separation of powers, sharing of powers, and federalism. In practice, as Carr would predict, these each prove to be more mythical than concrete. Nevertheless, they are important just the same.

The Myth of Majority Rule

Fundamental to *liberal* theory is the belief that the people should govern, and that government officials must abide by the will of the majority. And though the authors of the Constitution themselves strayed from early *liberal* thought with their distrust of the majority, majoritarian pressures were definitely exerted at the Constitutional Convention. According to the original document, the Constitution itself would be ratified by majority consent (of the men with voting privileges), members of the U.S. House of Representatives would be elected by a popular vote in each state, and the Constitution itself would be amended only by an overwhelming majority vote. Perhaps the founders recognized that when forcefully united, the voice of the people could not be ignored. But more importantly, *liberal* theory puts its faith in the majority; it assumes that majority opinion is more likely to reflect the self-evident truths of natural law than the often myopic vision of self-interested individuals.

Furthermore, throughout America's history, faith in majority rule has in many ways increased, leading, for example, to constitutional amendments effectively granting women and eighteen-year olds the right to vote and requiring members of the U.S. Senate to be chosen by popular vote. Indeed, contrary to the hopes of the founders, faith in the popular will has increasingly shaped the way presidential candidates seek and maintain office, altogether frustrating the founders' original aspirations for the Electoral College. Among federal institutions, only the Supreme Court remains partially isolated from the effects of the popular will, and even this institution has been compromised as popularly influenced presidents and senators appoint and approve its justices. Finally, belief in majority rule has recently resulted in the rise of the referendum process, by which a multitude of laws that elected representatives are unwilling to sponsor make it onto the ballot for popular approval. Ironically, even the term limit movement, which implies a lack of faith in the people's ability to vote out incumbents, is ultimately based on the perception that entrenched government officials are not responsive enough to the will of the majority.

The reliance on majority rule to control government further appears in the American ideal of freedom of speech and press. If the people are to govern, they must be informed, making freedom of speech and press vital to American liberty. Furthermore, the free press is considered to have a government "watchdog" role; as a result, American journalists enjoy tremendous access to government officials, including office space in the White House. Significantly, Americans consider foreign societies without a free press inherently undemocratic, in spite of any elections they might hold.

The importance of the majority rule ideal can also be seen in the way Americans view elections. Many mainstream Americans consider voting their most important act of citizenship. The right to vote symbolizes freedom, and voting is considered a civic and patriotic duty. Furthermore, political candidates take elections serious enough to spend countless millions of dollars on them. Finally, freedom of speech and the press as a check on government remains central to American political culture. Surely, of all ways to control government officials, the ideal of popular sovereignty gets the greatest amount of public attention.

But what happens when the ideal of majority rule is not respected? What happens when those in power manipulate elections or hide information from the press? How can we enforce the ideal of majority rule if our leaders are not interested in encouraging it? The logic of the Declaration of Independence implies that the people have no one to turn to but themselves when government consistently fails to respect their will. However true this is, it is also quite inconvenient for individuals to constantly monitor government. In short, majority rule is more useful as a unifying myth than as a practical method for day-to-day control of government officials.

More significantly still, the original drafters of the Constitution did not equate the ideal of popular sovereignty with the practice of majority vote at all. Though Jefferson himself seemed more committed to majority rule by actual voting, many of the founders considered popular sovereignty in an almost purely mythical way. Significantly, those who signed the Declaration did not ask for a majority vote to determine the true will of the people. Without even seeking a majority vote, they viewed themselves as acting on behalf of the People (with a capital P). Furthermore, the writers of the Constitution simply did not trust majorities. Only members of the U.S. House of Representatives were chosen by majority vote, and by today's standards, voting privileges were greatly limited. Moreover, the framers had little faith that elections could really hold government officials accountable. As those pushing for term limits understand, individuals seeking voter approval can easily manipulate the emotions of the electorate with slick campaign techniques, making the election process inadequate to insure that government officials conscientiously follow the will of the people. In short, the ideal of majority rule can play only a limited role, and the writers of the Constitution concentrated instead on mechanisms integral to the actual day-to-day workings of government to keep government officials within acceptable bounds.

Separation of Powers Myth

Anyone who has taken a high school government or civics class has been introduced to the concept of separation of powers. The ideal supposes that if separate powers are given to each branch of government, no government official could monopolize all power. This ideal was also inherited from Locke and other *liberal* revolutionaries. As Locke saw it, divine right theory allowed all governmental powers to be concentrated into far too few hands—leading inevitably to tyranny and abuse. Hence the problem Jefferson described in the Declaration: the King of Great Britain had taken all governmental powers to himself and as a result had become an unacceptable tyrant. By imagining governmental powers as separable, *liberal* theory posits a practical solution to this problem. And though we shall see that in practice, power separation is virtually impossible, the myth of separation of powers is an integral part of American political culture.

Legislative Power

American political theory conceives governmental powers into three distinct categories: legislative, executive, and judicial. The legislative power determines the law, arguably, the government's initial and most important power. Indeed, the U.S. Constitution implies as much. The section describing the legislative powers is the first and by far longest in the Constitution. A quick reading of Article One indicates that the Constitution grants tremendous legislative power to the U.S. Congress, including the power to collect taxes, raise armies, and regulate commerce. Furthermore, Article One seems to grant Congress almost unlimited authority to exercise its powers by stating explicitly that Congress has the power to "make all Laws which shall be necessary and proper for carrying into Execution" all the powers listed. Nevertheless, American political ideals actually envision the legislative powers of Congress to be quite limited. Article One starts with the phrase: "All legislative Powers herein granted

...," implying a prior power which is doing the granting, and we must look to the Preamble of the Constitution in order to fully appreciate how American political culture understands the proper legislative power granted Congress.

In typical classic *liberal* fashion, the Preamble of the Constitution states:

> We the People of the United States, in Order to form a more perfect Union, establish Justice, insure domestic Tranquility, provide for the common defense, promote the general Welfare, and secure the Blessings of Liberty to ourselves and our Posterity, do ordain and establish this Constitution for the United States of America.

The Preamble is consistent with *liberal* theory in that it suggests that the People, with a capital P, are ultimately in charge. It is the People who institute a Constitution in order to establish Justice, with a capital J, and to secure the Blessings of Liberty. In other words, underlying the Constitution and its grant of legislative power to Congress is the assumption that true Justice and Liberty exist prior to anything Congress might do. The Constitution is founded on the *liberal* assumption of natural law and the belief that only the People have the prerogative to determine whether or not government is living up to its responsibility to secure the Blessings of Liberty. The legitimate legislative power granted by the People to Congress extends no further.

How then, do the People determine when Congress is acting within its proper bounds? What mechanism do the People use to make their voice heard? Clearly it cannot be Congress. If the People existed prior to the creation of the Constitution, no governmental body created with the adoption of the Constitution can speak with the voice of the People. This is an issue we will return to later. For now, suffice it to say that the legislative power granted Congress is conceived from the start as being limited to that which the People, acting *outside* of Congress declare legitimate.

The Constitution also clearly envisions a legislative power distinct and separable from other government powers. The first sentence of Article One states: "All legislative Powers herein granted shall be vested in a Congress of the United States which shall consist of a Senate and House of Representatives." By separating the legislative power from the other powers of government, the authors of the Constitution hoped to insure that those making the law were not the same as those enforcing it, and vice versa. The term *all* is quite clear. All legislative power granted by the Constitution is vested in the Congress.

In practice, however, it is difficult to keep *all* legislative power in the hands of Congress and still govern effectively, because in order to do all the things it is expected to do, Congress must pass a tremendous amount of law. However, since the point of law is to secure the "Blessings of Liberty," any particular law that attempts to fit every situation will, in many cases, seem illegitimately constraining to many individuals. Consequently, Congress tends to pass general laws and looks to bureaucracies (which it also creates) to enforce the spirit of the general law by developing policies and procedures that seem appropriate. In doing so, Congress has clearly granted legislative power to un-elected bureaucrats who work in the executive branch. Obviously, this could be seen as a direct violation of the Constitution, yet in practice, it seems like there could be no other way. Members of Congress simply cannot write general laws with enough detail to make them effective, limited, and applicable to every situation. Those implementing the general principle of the law must have the capability to be flexible as they fill in many of the blanks.

Who then determines whether Congress has appropriately granted legislative power to executive officials? Are presidential executive orders, which effectively change the law, a violation of the Constitution? Or can Congress grant the president such power? If the president or any other member of the executive branch appears to be acting outside of the spirit of the general laws Congress has passed, does Congress have the Constitutional prerogative to stop them or does this power belong to someone else?

In practice, the U.S. Supreme Court has been called on to resolve these kinds of questions. However, as will become clear when we discuss the judicial power, resolving this kind of question is not part of the judicial power granted to the Court. In fact, if the judicial branch were granted this authority, the very principle of separation of powers would be violated. The truth is, American political mythology refuses to grant this power to any government institution. As stated above, the Preamble of the Constitution assumes a mythical People that exist prior to the Constitution. It is the People who are responsible for parceling out the respective powers to the various institutions of government and, theoretically, only the People can resolve disputes between branches. The problem is, the People have no clear and indisputable method for making its will known, and these sorts of questions are ultimately never fully resolved. But this is an issue we will have to return to. For now, it is enough to recognize that though the Constitution is clear in stating that all legislative power is granted to Congress, it is impossible for Congress to do its job effectively without parceling some of that power out—making it necessary for someone to keep an eye on Congress.

Executive Power

American political culture requires that the executive power, the power to execute the law, also be understood as distinctly different and separable from the legislative power. Congress only makes law—for the mechanism to work, it must be completely dependent on others to carry out the laws it makes. Ideally, this arrangement insures that legislators are subject to the laws they pass, discouraging them from making laws by which they themselves would not want to abide and prevents those executing the law from making partial, arbitrary, and self-serving laws. With this ideal in mind, critics accuse presidents who use executive orders to "make law" of over-stepping their bounds. Article Two of the Constitution sets up a completely separate executive branch and does not grant presidents this kind of power.

As argued above, however, the separation of the executive from the legislative power has proven to be elusive. It is virtually impossible for Congress to pass laws specific enough for all situations; those enforcing the laws must fill in the details. Furthermore, American political mythology actually embraces the concept of executive prerogative.

In lengthy discussion of executive prerogative, Locke concludes that such prerogative is a necessary power of the chief *executive* officer because legislative bodies are not always in session, and as deliberative bodies, are incapable of swift action. Locke reasoned that as long as the executive was acting to preserve the will of the People, it was a proper and even necessary exercise of *executive* powers to use prerogative, even to the point, when the situation called for it, of opposing a specific law passed by the legislature. Significantly, Locke viewed this as an executive power and not a legislative one. When exercising prerogative correctly, the chief executive, in Locke's view, does not make law at all. How is this so?

Once again we face the significant logic of the Declaration and Preamble. The legislative power delineated in the Constitution is granted by the People only to secure the "Blessings of Liberty." But because the rights of the People exist according to the laws of nature, prior to the Constitution, the primary responsibility of the executive lies in executing laws of nature that exist prior to Congress. As Jefferson indicated, legitimate government must operate within the self-evident bounds prescribed by nature, and it is ultimately the chief executive's responsibility to execute this *natural law*. Ideally, Congressional legislation will harmonize with natural law. But if it does not, executive actions must trump it. In this way, conservatives willing to overlook a Republican president's use of executive orders while being critical of Democratic Presidents for doing the same thing are not necessarily hypocritical. As long as they believe Republicans are acting in accordance with the true will of the People, American political mythology informs them that presidential prerogative is appropriate and necessary.

Thus President Lincoln responded quickly to the hostile acts of southerners without Congressional consent and without a declaration of war. Thus the Reagan administration justified ignoring a specific act of Congress to provide funds for the Contra terrorist activities in Nicaragua. As long as presidents are enforcing what they consider the real will of the People, the prerogative is a proper executive function.

But again, the big question is how to determine whether a given exercise of executive prerogative harmonizes with natural law. One person's legitimate executive prerogative is another's violation of separation of powers. Who speaks for the People in this extra-constitutional way? Significantly, Jefferson did not look to a government institution to declare that the King of Great Britain was violating the People's trust. This power exists prior to and outside of government institutions. We will return to this shortly; for now, it is sufficient to recognize that in American political culture, the executive power is not limited to enforcing the laws passed by the legislature. The executive power includes the power to execute natural law in order to secure the "Blessings of Liberty" that pre-date Congress.

Judicial Power

There is perhaps more confusion about the judicial power in American political culture than about any other governmental power. Under the separation of powers logic, the proper judicial power is not, as so many contemporary conservatives argue, the power to interpret the law. Though judges must often interpret law in order to carry out their function, so too must members of the executive branch. It is impossible to implement and enforce a law based on broad principles without first interpreting it. For example, a law that makes it a crime to disturb the peace must first be interpreted by any police officer prior to making an arrest. And though the officer's interpretation of the law can be overturned by a judge's interpretation, interpreting the law is not the uniquely judicial function anticipated by the separation of powers logic. In fact, the common conservative argument that "judges should interpret and not make law" does not make any sense in the context of the separation of powers doctrine. Surely the power to *interpret* law is the power to *make* law, insofar as interpreting determines what the law actually means. In short, conservatives are correct in perceiving that judges often exercise legislative power. But if they sincerely do not want judges making law, conservatives should rethink the argument that a judge's responsibility is to interpret the law.[29]

Nor is it correct to suggest that the proper judicial power, under the separation of powers logic, is to determine the constitutionality of law. This power, though often exercised by the judiciary, ultimately amounts to the power to make law and is therefore also a legislative power. In short, under the separation of powers logic, the power to make law in any form—writing law, interpreting the law, or determining its constitutionality, is the legislative power. Regardless of what we might call it, any government body that determines what the law ultimately means and which laws will be applied is exercising legislative power. That entity is establishing the law.

So, if there are indeed three separate governmental powers, the judicial power must be something completely different from the power to determine the meaning and constitutionality of law. The separation of powers ideal does in fact conceive of such a power. Judicial power is the power to insure fair execution of the law. That is, the judicial power checks those who enforce the law, not those who make it. In short, the separation-of-powers ideal envisions three distinct

[29] Even when Supreme Court justices rule that an act of Congress is unconstitutional, they see themselves as interpreting the Constitution. So it makes no sense for critics of an activist Court to argue that the Court's role is to merely interpret the law.

powers: the power to make law, the power to enforce the law that has been made, and the power to insure that the enforcement of law is impartial and fair.

In other words, the judicial power is limited to judging the actions of executive officials exclusively. In this sense, the judicial power only comes into play with regard to the actions of *particular* government executives towards *particular* individuals. Contemporary conservatives are correct in suggesting that every time the Court rules on the legitimacy of a law in general as opposed to a *particular* way of *enforcing* that law, it is exercising *legislative* and not judicial power.

In a nutshell, then, the separation-of-powers ideal envisions the following scenario: the legislative power determines the speed limit, raising all the issues and making all the arguments needed to make this determination. Once the determination is made, the legislative activity ends, until the legislative body itself determines to take up the question again. The executive branch arrests individuals driving over the speed limit, and its power ends there. To question the wisdom of the speed limit is not the responsibility of the executive officer. And finally, judicial power hears the pleas of all individuals claiming to have been wrongfully arrested. However, before the judge, the claims of such individuals must be limited to questioning the actions of the police officer and not the legislature. The judicial power determines *only* whether the police officer was enforcing the law. A judge who entertains questions regarding the legitimacy of the speed limit would be to engaging in the legislative function.

In practice it is much more convoluted. If, for example, the legislature determines that the speed limit is 55 miles per hour, police officers might reasonably determine that, given limited resources to enforce the law, they will allow people to actually drive 58 miles per hour without stopping them. In doing so, these officers clearly exercise legislative power, because they determine what speed limit will actually be enforced, and governments can do very little to prevent officers from doing so. The legislature can try to rein in errant officers by threatening to cut off funding for the police department, but ultimately, the officer on duty must decide which laws to enforce with what degree of exactitude.

If the same police officer arrests one individual for driving 58 miles per hour while ignoring many others doing the same, it would be an exercise of judicial power to determine whether the police officer was being arbitrary in making the arrest. In practice, more times than not the police officer alone makes this determination as well, as most speeding violations are not challenged in court. When this happens, clearly the myth of separation of powers has completely broken down. The officer on duty has had the sole opportunity to exercise all three powers.

Practical necessity thus demands that individuals executing the law need the kind of flexibility described above, and the ideal of separation of powers must, in fact, remain more a myth than an institutionalized reality. Government could not function if it kept these powers as separate as the ideal suggests. This is made even more evident by the fact that many laws passed by the legislature are necessarily less precise than a 55 mile per hour speed limit. Many laws are more akin to a law that simply states: "Drive Reasonably." In this situation, police officers have no choice but to exercise legislative powers and determine what the term *reasonable* means. In the rare case that an arresting officer's judgment is actually challenged and taken to court, the judge must also exercise legislative power before judicial power can even be invoked. The judge must first interpret the meaning of the term "Drive Reasonably." In this situation, the judge determines the law and the judge's exercise of legislative power is final. So in the rare situation that the police officer is not the sole person exercising all three powers, the judge, and *not* the legislature, has the final legislative responsibility, once again violating separation of powers.

The Actual Role of the Separation of Powers Myth

Given that the ideal of separation of powers cannot in practice be precisely followed, why does it remain an integral element of American political culture? The answer lies in the passage from the *Federalist Papers* referred to at the beginning of this chapter. Government officials need extensive powers to control individuals with a natural proclivity towards selfishness. Yet government officials themselves must also be controlled. The ideal of separation of powers makes the possibility for doing both very real. Tremendous powers are legitimately granted, and even though they are never separated as neatly as the ideal suggests, there is a perceived limit to the legitimate powers of any executive, legislative, or judicial officer. In short, the ideal works to provide a check on official activities even though it is just an ideal. Though executive officials do need to exercise all three powers to function effectively, it would be tyranny indeed if their actions could not be challenged. The myth of separation of powers plays a crucial role in making this possible. Government officials can be effective only when they have legitimacy in the eyes of the people they govern. The separation of powers ideal helps keep official actions inside acceptable bounds.[30]

We have yet to return to the big question of who ultimately decides when Congress or the president or the courts have violated the separation of powers principle. Nor can we yet fully answer this question. The U.S. Supreme Court has often been called on to do so, though as our discussion of the judicial power suggests, this power is clearly not part of the proper judicial power as understood by the separation of powers doctrine. Indeed, to grant this kind of power to any

---

[30] As mentioned above, Carr argued that this interaction between actual practice and ideals is the stuff of politics. Ideals keep practice in check. This seems to suggest that true belief in the possibility of the ideal would be necessary for this dynamic to function. In other words, widespread understanding that ideals are never actually realized might undermine the efficacy of ideals altogether, and I should celebrate the fact that this book will never become a best seller. Determining if this assumption is true is beyond the scope of this text, as it would involve a deep examination of the human psyche. Can ideals have the same efficacy even when we openly know they are just myths? Perhaps. Few adults believe in Santa Claus yet the Santa myth still seems capable of greatly shaping behavior.

single government institution would be to violate the very separation of powers principle. Consequently, whenever the Court has participated in this function, it has invited condemnation. In theory, only the People (with a capital P,) who stand outside and above the Constitution and the government institutions and practices created by it, have this power.

And with this power comes the real source of the problem. For classic *liberal* theory operates in the name of the People, yet there is no clear mechanism for the People to clearly and *irrefutably* make itself heard. Congress, though made up of representatives elected by the people, is understood to be capable of violating the People's trust. Presidents, though entrusted with the power of prerogative to act for the People, are clearly equally capable of violating this trust. So is the Supreme Court. Nor are elections the solution. As stated earlier, the People that Jefferson referred to in the Declaration, who appear in the Preamble of the Constitution, represent a concept greater than the principle of majority rule. Jefferson did not call for an election to determine if a revolution was needed. Nor did Lincoln call for a vote before acting to save the Union.

In the end, then, the ideal of separation of powers is problematic because no individual or institution responsible is clearly for determining whether or not it is being violated. But this problem requires no solution. In fact, the opposite is true. As Chapter One concluded, just as contradicting political ideals work against tyranny by keeping all political positions somewhat off balance, so too does the inability to decisively determine when power has been misappropriated. This is the greatest value of the separation of powers myth. No government entity can act for too long without appearing to violate the ideal, and rather than resolving this dilemma, our greatest challenge is preserving the myth in the face of the hard reality that it can never be practiced.

As I suggested in Chapter One and will argue in Chapter Five, the Supreme Court is uniquely positioned to play a major role in the preservation of American political mythology, including the ideal of separation of powers. In fact, I claim that preserving American mythology is the Court's essential role—even though this responsibility lies outside of any power specifically granted it by the U.S. Constitution and is clearly greater than the exercise of its judicial power. But this is the topic of another chapter. First we must briefly examine the ideal of sharing powers as another check against government excess.

The Myth of Sharing Powers

At first blush, the ideal of sharing powers may seem to contradict the ideal of separating powers. If powers are separated, how can they simultaneously be shared? Indeed, to the degree that American political culture expects sharing of powers to help avoid tyranny, such sharing conflicts with the separation of powers myth. Nevertheless, both are clearly at work in American political culture and though some of the apparent contradictions can be reasoned away, in the end it must be acknowledged that Americans depend on contradictory ideals to insure control over government.

One way to understand the ideal of power sharing is to trace it to *liberal* theory's argument that no individual should judge his/her own situation. Under pure separation of powers myth, this would not be the case. Legislators would have sole power to legislate, executive officials would have sole power to execute, and judicial officers would have sole authority to adjudicate. Though under pure separation of powers no one would be capable of exercising powers outside of their realm, there would be no ability for an outside body to insure that the powers allocated to specific institutions were being used fully and properly. For example, even though the judiciary can insure that executive officials do not act arbitrarily against particular individuals, judges cannot insure that the executive branch actually executes the law that has been passed. In short, one way to conceive of the sharing of powers logic, while remaining semi-consistent to the ideal of power separation, is to view power sharing as the power of *oversight* and power separation as the power of *initial action*.

I argued above that much power sharing comes about out of necessity. The powers of government cannot be separated in practice as easily as they can be in theory. Congress, for example, cannot anticipate every individual situation and must pass broad laws that define general principles, then ask those enforcing the law to fill in the details for particular situations. This inevitably results in the executive branch making most law—presumably within the guidelines Congress has provided. Furthermore, the judicial branch largely determines which details provided by the executive branch are legitimate. And if Congress disagrees with the way the courts have interpreted the law they initially passed, they can always revisit it, making their intentions much more explicit. Thus, in practice, all three branches are heavily involved with the legislative power and in this way provide a constant check on each other.

Furthermore, the sharing of powers was created by design. For example, though Section One of Article One of the Constitution grants *all* legislative power to Congress, Section Seven requires that all legislation be subject to a presidential veto. This veto power is also best understood as an oversight power. Congress must initiate all legislation, and the president's veto can be overridden. What the veto does is to insure that a potentially controversial law has strong legislative support.

Similarly, Congress is granted power to oversee the executive branch because it controls the purse strings and can pass new directives. Executive officials defying the will of Congress may find their funds removed. Congress also has constitutional power to impeach executive and judicial officials, insuring that no individual can be free from some sort of oversight.

However, we cannot include the U.S. Supreme Court's practice of ruling on the constitutionality of congressional laws as part of the sharing of powers logic. Though this practice has come to be accepted as a major responsibility of the Court, it must not be understood as a routine oversight function. To grant the Court this power explicitly would be to throw the separation of powers ideal greatly out of balance—concentrating too much power in the hands of one governmental body. Indeed the Court exercises this power only because it seems like it must for reasons much different than those required in a typical oversight function. But this conclusion cannot be pursued just yet. For now, it is enough to recognize that in American political culture, judicial overturning of acts of Congress involves much more than legislative oversight.

The Myth of Federalism

The final major ideal that American political mythology embraces to control government officials is federalism. Similar to separation of powers, federalism also envisions governmental powers divided into separate, virtually impenetrable spheres. Only federalism separates powers in altogether different ways. From this view, the Constitution was adopted to grant the national government authority to govern in areas that require cooperation of all state governments while reserving all other governmental powers to respective state governments. Under federalism, the national government has exclusive authority in its realm and state governments have exclusive authority in theirs. American political culture views national governmental powers as being distinct and clearly delineated. Article Two of the Constitution includes a precise list of legislative powers granted to the national government. This list is considered complete, for the Tenth Amendment pronounces "all powers not delegated to the United States by the Constitution ... are reserved to the States respectively, or to the people." In sum, federalism requires state governments to comply with legitimate national government authority, but it also tells the national government what its exact boundaries are. Under federalism, national government and state governments alike must abide by the constitutional limits placed on them.

As you may have probably guessed, in practice, this ideal has also proven impossible to institutionalize. And again, the root of the problem is the absence of an arbitrator clearly authorized to settle disputes. Once powers and responsibilities are divided between separate sovereign entities, who has the legitimate authority to determine when one of the entities is violating the sovereignty of another? More importantly, when the national government oversteps its bounds, who has the authority, or ability to stop it? At its peak, the inability to resolve these issues resulted in the Civil War. Southern leaders were convinced that they could no longer rely on national government officials to uphold the terms of the Constitution—including its protection of their right to continue the practice of slavery. Yet to whom could they turn and demand that the national government live up to its end of the Constitution? When it mattered most, federalism proved to be a cruel illusion, and just as Thomas Jefferson considered it his duty to throw off the British Crown, these leaders came to see it as their right, indeed their obligation, to secede from the Union.

Following the Civil War, the Thirteenth, Fourteenth, and Fifteenth, Amendments were passed as a means for establishing American citizenship for former slaves, and as a means to insure that state governments would not violate individual rights of citizens. Prior to the passage of the Fourteenth Amendment, the U.S. Constitution's Bill of Rights applied only to the national government. With the passage of the Fourteenth, state governments in a sense became as bound as the national government to preserve the self-evident "Blessings of Liberty" of the People. But the Civil War Amendments were not intended to end the principle of federalism, and even with its passage, state governments retained all legitimate powers not granted to the national government. However, just as the national government has a difficult time acting without seeming to violate some individual's unalienable right (see Chapter One,) so too are state governments often perceived as encroaching on individual liberties. When this happens, who is responsible for determining when a state government is acting unconstitutionally? Just as no government institution has the theoretical authority to tell Congress that its legislation violates the laws of nature, no government authority can tell state governments when they have overstepped their bounds.

In practice, these questions have also been appealed to the U.S. Supreme Court. Nevertheless, it would be an exaggeration to say that this practice has settled the matter. Indeed the Court cannot even hear these issues without appearing to violate the very principle of federalism. Federalism demands that as an institution of the national government, the U.S. Supreme Court stay out of state issues. If states are acting within their constitutional limits, no federal entity, including the Supreme Court, can legitimately interfere. And as critics of an "activist" Court claim, the Fourteenth Amendment does not change this. In short, to grant the U.S. Supreme Court authority to determine whether or not states are upholding the Constitution is to negate the very principle of federalism.

However, state governments have historically been quite willing to violate individual liberties including the right to free speech, freedom to worship, and the right to privacy. From this perspective, the whole point of the Fourteenth Amendment was to insure individual freedoms against state interference. If the national government cannot demand that state governments preserve these liberties, why did we pass the Fourteenth Amendment in the first place? Consequently, even as federalism demands that the U.S. federal courts stay out of state affairs, it demands that U.S. federal courts protect individuals from state abuse. And so, yet again, the big question is, who decides when the U.S. federal courts are acting within their realm and when they are overstepping their bounds?

Similarly, state officials occasionally accuse the U.S. government of violating the Constitution by exercising power reserved to the states. Although in practice states look to the U.S. Supreme Court on such occasions, they do so grudgingly and only as a matter of practical necessity—there is nowhere else to turn. The ideal of federalism grants no governmental body the theoretical authority to hear such a claim. And since the U.S. Supreme Court is part of the national government, asking it to settle these questions is literally asking the national government to control itself—something the very ideal of federalism is meant to avoid. In sum, critics of "judicial activism" are correct in perceiving that federalism's reliance on the Supreme Court puts it on shaky ground. The revolutionary colonists did not take King George to a British court, which is the equivalent of what state government officials do when they ask the U.S. Supreme Court to protect them from an over zealous U.S. government.

There is no easy resolution to this problem. It clearly cannot be found in the Constitution. Though the Constitution states that the U.S. Constitution is the supreme law of the land, this is obviously no solution. American political mythology considers U.S. government officials no less likely than state government officials to violate the Constitution. And once again, American political theory conceives that the only real authority over these matters is the People.

The colonists did not sue King George in one of his own courts when they felt his government was in violation of natural law. Individuals, acting in the name of "the People," took matters into their own hands. And, as the Preamble to the Constitution suggests, it was the People who, by establishing the Constitution, parceled out certain responsibilities for the national government and left others for state governments. Consequently the People alone have the legitimate authority to settle disputes. Yet it is difficult for the People to do so clearly and irrefutably. So, although critics correctly assert that reliance on the courts ultimately undermines the legitimate power of the People, there may be no other alternative short of violent revolution.

In sum, like the ideals of separation of power and power sharing, the concept of federalism, with its belief in separate sovereign governments, can only exist as a mythical ideal—practice demands that one government entity exercise final authority over others. Nevertheless, the founder's faith in federalism and their unwillingness or inability to resolve its contradictions is once again part of the desirable richness of American political culture. More important than the resolution of this conflict is the belief in federalism. Respect for the ideal helps keep both state and national governments from clearly and indisputably claiming sole power.

Preserving this respect is much more important than resolving any particular dispute between state and national governments. At the time of the Civil War, the ideal itself was in jeopardy in the eyes of Southern leaders. They were convinced that national government officials did not respect the principle of federalism and saw no other way to preserve their constitutionally guaranteed freedoms but to secede. In that situation, the sheer force of Union soldiers eventually resolved the issue. To those who supported secession in the South, the rules forced upon them immediately following the war were no more legitimate than the rule of King George in the eyes of Thomas Jefferson. And though secession may no longer appear to be a realistic option with today's powerful national military, the legitimacy of all governments—both state and national, will be greater insofar as the ideal of federalism is respected.

Again, the U.S. Supreme Court is uniquely positioned to encourage the preservation of this respect, and critics of the Court's activism may want to reconsider the nature of their most vocal complaints. Judicial activism per se is not the problem. Having in practice become the government institution with the final authority to resolve questions of national and state sovereignty, the U.S. Supreme Court has no choice but to act. As all Court watchers clearly understood in the highly visible *Bush* v. *Gore* presidential election case, once the Court is called upon to act, non-action itself is action. Furthermore, in this case, those normally concerned with judicial activism were quite sincere in their desire that the U.S. Supreme Court would act, suggesting that the question of judicial activism itself is not the real issue. The real issue facing the U.S. Supreme Court, the issue that contemporary liberals and conservatives alike were passionately moved by, is the Court's obligation to *appear* committed to the ideals of federalism. In these cases, whatever the Court decides, it must above all *appear* to be bigger than its actual national-government-institution self. If the Court appears to be just another powerful, politically driven, U.S. government institution, respect for the very ideal of federalism is jeopardized, and the Court has failed to meet this most important obligation.

Conclusion

By starting with the assumption that individuals are naturally endowed with unalienable rights threatened by excessive government, American political culture considers government's biggest challenge to be is keeping itself under control. The founders attempted to meet this challenge by dividing state power from national power, creating separate legislative, executive, and judicial branches, each sharing legislative, executive, and judicial powers, and finally granting majorities the power of the vote. Yet, after all this, American political mythology envisions first and foremost a natural law that stands above all these institutions. This conception makes it impossible for any single government institution to legitimately claim final authority to resolve disputes between institutions. The founders could not grant this authority to any institution without violating the very principle they were trying to establish. But more importantly, the theory of natural individual rights ultimately does not grant this authority to any government institution. This authority is the province of mythical natural law.

According to the theory implicit in the Declaration of Independence, all legitimate law is circumscribed by self-evident, even God-given, natural law. The responsibility of government is to enforce this law and to go no further. Powers are separated, shared, and divided all with this goal in mind. Legitimate government must remain within the bounds of natural law. However, the founders also believed that government is necessary due to the human tendency to violate natural law. This assumption ultimately creates an irresolvable dilemma. Since no individual can be trusted to enforce natural law, no government official or institution can be trusted with this power either. The very purpose of government is to keep any single individual or institution (including the Supreme Court) from having final authority, and American political culture will always suffer from a potential crisis of authority. In short, the contradictory demands of these ideals cooperate (often unintentionally) to keep governmental tyranny at bay. No government institution is immune from careful scrutiny.

However, unless Americans are willing to rely on violent revolutions on a regular basis, there is a clear *political* need for an accepted final authority. In practice, some authority short of natural law must be allowed to determine when these principles are being violated. Some institution must be seen as having the authority to insure that natural law prevails and the "Blessings of Liberty" preserved.

The U.S. Supreme Court has inherited this responsibility. Although this is not a part of the judicial power explicitly granted to it by the Constitution, the Court has come to be viewed as having this particular power. Consequently, much of the criticism leveled at the Court's activism is misplaced. Having inherited the final authority to resolve questions of national and state sovereignty, the U.S. Supreme Court has no choice but to exercise judicial activism. Once called upon, the Court must exercise this power and must go beyond simply *interpreting* the law. The very fact that it can accept or reject cases that raise these constitutional questions of authority makes it so. Its law-making power is felt, even when it refuses to act.

Yet the practical necessity for a final authority does not negate the equally practical importance of the ideal demanding that no government institution have this kind of authority, putting the Court in a precarious situation in many cases. In typical "damned if you do, damned if you don't" fashion, the Court cannot help but be seen as acting tyrannically every time it is called upon to settle a constitutional question.

The point of this chapter, however, is not to commiserate with the Court and silence its critics, but more importantly, to question the nature of their criticism. For though the ideals we have examined cannot be realized in practice, this does not lessen their importance. On the contrary, these ideals must be celebrated and every effort must be taken to insure that they are preserved and respected.

As the institution entrusted with the final authority over constitutional questions, the real issue facing the U.S. Supreme Court is its obligation to *appear* committed to the mythical ideals of majority rule, separation of powers, sharing of powers, and federalism. In such cases, the Court's mythical role is its most important role. Whatever the Court decides, it is imperative that it *appear* to transcend its institutional identity. Indeed, to act at all, the Court *must* violate the very principles of majority rule, separation of powers, sharing of powers, and federalism, making it very vulnerable to criticism. But the real question the Court's critics should consider is whether the Court has done its best to preserve a healthy belief in these myths even as it is required to violate them. This is the topic of the final chapter. Before going there, we must gain a deeper understanding of American political mythology by examining a different set of ideals altogether.

Papa Knows Best

Chapter Three
The Myths of Republicanism

To this point, I have focused almost exclusively on the classic *liberal* elements of American political culture. I have argued that the *liberal* assumption of self-evident, unalienable individual rights makes powerful yet contradictory claims on American government. In particular, I have argued that building on a foundation of individual rights, *liberal* mythology conceives of a government whose sole purpose is to preserve those rights. Absent is any concept that the government has a responsibility to the public as a public. Furthermore, this view of government makes it difficult for government to act without being perceived as violating some individual's freedom, and exposes all government activity to constant questioning. Chapter One argued that Democrats and Republicans share these ideals, that most conflict between these parties can be explained as the result of the contradictions in the ideals themselves, and that these contradictions constitute the very strength of American politics, providing a check on all political activity regardless of the party in power. In Chapter Two, we examined how the *liberal* emphasis on individual rights has resulted in contradictory theories of government, which in turn have kept government officials within certain boundaries. Unworkable as they may be, I concluded, the ideals of separation of powers, sharing of powers, majority rule and federalism challenge the legitimacy of many government activities—once again adding to the health of American politics and providing a needed check on the use of power. As complex as this is, however, this portrait of American political culture remains substantially incomplete. For in spite of the virtual omnipresence of *liberal* ideals, there is another side to American political culture yet to be examined. This other side comes complete with its own set of ideals that are in direct conflict with American *liberalism*—a conflict that is reflected in the very names of the dominant competing political parties.

Earlier it was indicated that the founders were not in complete agreement with *liberal* mythology, particularly regarding Locke's faith in the majority. I suggested that their concept of the "People" did not equate with Locke's principle of majority rule, and that many founders were highly suspicious of a mass majority. Moreover, for those present at the Constitutional Convention in Philadelphia, disagreements with Locke did not end with that skepticism and the theory of government that best represents many of their ideals is not Lockean *liberalism* at all—rather, it is the theory of republicanism.

Contrary to *liberal* theory, republicanism asserts that the purpose of government is to promote the good of the republic, as opposed to the individual, that the good of the republic is best understood by a selective few individuals, as opposed to the popular majority, and that virtue, or the ability to sacrifice self for the good of the group, as opposed to enlightened self-interest, is necessary for a healthy society. Furthermore, republicanism values the rule of law, as opposed to popular sovereignty. Significantly, republican mythology is not just different from *liberalism*—it is in direct opposition to it. Moreover, though it could be said that in some ways the Democratic Party promotes the *liberal* ideals of individual rights and majority rule, while the Republican Party believes more republicanism, it would be a mistake to push this distinction too far. Neither party has a monopoly on either mythology. Successful candidates in both parties find it necessary to adhere to both sets of contradicting ideals simultaneously.

In this chapter we will examine republican mythology in detail to see how its ideals add to the richness of American political culture. Once again, it will be argued that, inconsistent as these ideals are with the aforementioned American political ideals, their preservation is imperative. The U.S. Supreme Court is uniquely positioned to preserve them.

Republicanism and the Myth of Machiavellian Virtue

Where *liberal* theory (assuming that "men are not angels") puts its faith in barriers designed to control self-seeking government officials, republicanism asserts the necessity for virtuous individuals. And, though in Chapter Two it was argued that the men-are-not-angels assumption of *Federalist No. 51* resulted in the principles of separation of powers, sharing of powers, and federalism, a more thorough reading of the *Federalist Papers* provides an altogether contrasting picture—one that highly values *virtue* and considers securing virtuous leaders to be the most important challenge of government:

> The aim of every political constitution is, or ought to be, first to obtain for rulers men who possess most wisdom to discern, and most virtue to pursue, the common good of the society; and in the next place, to take the most effectual precautions for keeping them virtuous whilst they continue to hold their public trust. *Federalist Papers No. 57*

The perceived need for encouraging virtue is a dominant theme throughout the *Federalist Papers*—completely opposing the classic *liberal* faith in the selfishness of the butcher and the baker. Furthermore, this theme rejects the skeptical realism of *liberal* theory with its distrust of altruism, and criticizes the self-serving politician and citizen alike. In short, the perceived need for virtue takes a view of human nature diametrically opposed to that of Locke and Smith.

This call for virtuous leadership goes as far back as Plato. But Florentine political philosopher Niccolo Machiavelli perhaps best expressed the ideal on display in American political culture. Machiavelli is often known in American circles for arguing cynically that the end justifies the means. To be "Machiavellian" is to disregard common morality in pursuit of one's political agenda. However, a deep reading of Machiavelli's *Discourses* provides a clearer picture of the ideal of virtue present in the American republican ideal. For Machiavelli, virtue demands the ability to sacrifice self, short-term political interests, and even inappropriate law, for the long-term good of the republic. He was convinced that this alone could save a people from the destructive forces of unrestrained selfishness. Consequently, Machiavelli encouraged political leaders to take matters into their own hands, only insofar as they acted for the good of the group and the health of the republic. This way of thinking was very much in the minds of the founders and remains a part of American political culture today. In many of our myths and stories, the end truly does justify the means.

For example, in pledging "our Lives our Fortunes and our sacred Honor" in support of the Declaration of Independence and in the name of "the good People of these Colonies," the signors of the Declaration displayed a belief in the necessity for Machiavellian virtue. Similarly, by violating the law and showing complete disregard for private property, those participating in the "Boston Tea Party" displayed a belief in the necessity for Machiavellian virtue. And indeed the fact that American political mythology celebrates the Boston Tea Party as a heroic act, where men of virtue risked their lives for the good of the nation, as opposed to seeing it as a vile, secretive disregard for private property, suggests the prevalence of this ideal. Indeed the approving portrayal of the Constitutional Convention itself, where men met in secret and plotted to replace the existing Articles of Confederation, clearly celebrates this Machiavellian virtue.

In Machiavelli's mind, few individuals had sufficient virtue to govern, and his ideal is elitist and paternalistic. It envisions aggressive leaders, willing to step out and lead, and receptive masses, willing to fall in and follow. This is a common element of the American republican ideal, one that will be examined in the next section. However, the American belief in virtue is not always so exclusive and often takes on a more democratic tone. When President Kennedy urged Americans "ask not what your country can do for you, but what you can do for your country," he called on all American citizens (not just a small elite) to be virtuous. In fact, American patriotism itself is a broad democratic celebration of the ideal of virtue. Moreover, patriotic passion itself completely flies in the face of Locke's reason and his emphasis on individual rights. Indeed, by claiming that the sole purpose of government rationally considered is to preserve individual freedom, *liberal* mythology has a hard time explaining why a soldier should "die for one's country." The republican ideal of virtue, meanwhile, celebrates this as the ultimate act of patriotism.

Significantly, the republican ideal of virtuous self-sacrifice is not the equivalent of *liberalism's* enlightened self-interest. *Liberal* theory assumes that the best interest of the individual is in harmony with the best interest of all individuals. Rational individuals subject themselves to the rules of the majority because they know they would be worse off with no government whatsoever. *Liberalism* fails to conceive that individuals can be required by government to sacrifice self. In those rare cases when government does require individuals to alter their behavior, *liberalism* considers such alterations in the individuals' best interest. In short, *liberal* mythology can expect a person to risk life for self, but not for country per se. The republican ideal of virtue, on the other hand, suggests a need to alter individual behavior for the good of the group, even at the expense of the individual. This ideal assumes, then, that personal sacrifice is needed to hold societies together, as opposed to rational calculations of one's long-term best interest. In short, the republican ideal exhorts individuals to rise above the what's-in-it-for-me attitude that *liberalism* champions.

As an example of both ideals coming into direct conflict, consider the severe turmoil America experienced over the Vietnam War. The republican ideal informs all citizens that they have a duty to pursue a higher cause, even if it means risking their own lives. On their return home, soldiers who marched to this ideal and risked everything for a cause greater than themselves, had a hard time comprehending why they were not welcomed as heroes, but were instead considered guilty for obeying their government and performing their duty. On the other hand, the *liberal* ideal reflected in the Declaration of Independence tells would-be draftees that a government that would sacrifice their lives for its own questionable ends is illegitimate, and that citizens have a moral obligation to disobey such a government at all costs. From this perspective, soldiers who took their marching orders from Washington were not unlike the treasonous colonists who sympathized with the British during the Revolutionary War, cowards, even traitors to justice, who certainly did not deserve a hero's welcome.

In Chapter Two, it was suggested that individuals who are most blinded by personal ambition are often the ones most likely to seek higher office, and that by making selfishness a virtue, *liberal* theory makes it difficult to find self-sacrificing leadership when it is really needed. Similarly, the Vietnam example suggest the republican ideal of virtue is also problematic, for it appeals to passions impervious to rational critique, and demands a degree of certitude that one's cause is greater than self and hence not subject to rational argument. This kind of thinking no doubt helps unite a nation and overcome the endemic selfishness of *liberalism*, but it also encourages uncritical demagoguery. Indeed perhaps the challenge to American political culture ignited by the Vietnam War indicates a healthy competition between two equally powerful ideals.

The Republican Myth and Paternalism

As stated above, Machiavelli's ideal of virtue was elitist and paternalistic. He was convinced that few had the virtue and courage necessary to govern well. He envisioned the need for assertive individuals with vision, who had the will and courage their subjects lacked to lead a mass of people. In the discussion of the ideal of representation in Chapter One, it was noted that those who signed the Declaration exhibited this kind of paternalism by viewing themselves as the representatives of "the good People" of the colonies. Similarly, it was shown that the preamble to the Constitution speaks for "We the People of the United States," even though nothing like a majority of the people living in the United States wrote and ratified that document, but rather people who saw themselves as representing what was best for the United States. Similarly, it was suggested that American presidents have viewed themselves as representing the enlightened will of the people.

Americans further express this ideal in their acceptance of "executive privilege," allowing countless government documents and activities to remain hidden from public view. Indeed, so strong was the American belief that leaders who knew best should be trusted to carry out the every day workings of government, that after his visit to America, Tocqueville envisioned a kind of despotism Americans might some day come to accept:

> In the first place, I see an innumerable multitude of men, alike and equal, constantly circling around in pursuit of the petty and banal pleasures with which they glut their souls. ...
>
> Over this kind of men stands an immense, protective power which is alone responsible for securing their enjoyment and watching over their fate. That power is absolute, thoughtful of detail, orderly, provident, and gentle. It would resemble parental authority if, father-like, it tried to prepare its charges for a man's life, but on the contrary, it only tries to keep them in perpetual childhood. It likes to see the citizens enjoy themselves, provided that they think of nothing but enjoyment. It gladly works for their happiness but wants to be sole agent and judge of it. It provides for their security, foresees and supplies their necessities, facilitates their pleasures, manages their principal concerns, directs their industry, makes rules for their testaments, and divides their inheritances. Why should it not entirely relieve them from the trouble of thinking and all the cares of living?[31]

To be sure, this level of passivity does not yet characterize America, yet at times Tocqueville's vision seems most prophetic. However, as bleak as this conception might seem, the republican ideal that calls for leadership is a valid one. Government officials too willing to listen to the majority have a difficult time setting priorities. Tax cuts coupled with deficit spending on government

---

[31] Tocqueville, p. 691-92.

programs are the results of politicians too focused on getting re-elected to step out and lead. Often what are critically needed are courageous leaders willing to stand against individual self-interest and the tides of an overzealous majority. The question is: how do you get strong leadership without the negative effects Tocqueville envisioned? There seems to be nothing in the republican paternalistic ideal that would fully prevent such effects.

Once again, the indispensable richness of American political culture, with its contradicting ideals, becomes evident. Perhaps the best way fully to guard against the negative aspects of republican paternalism while preserving its vital elements is simultaneously to embrace a completely contradictory ideal. Perhaps what best insures against unwanted paternalism while allowing for necessary leadership is the presence of the opposing Lockean *liberal* ideal. By suggesting that individuals have a moral obligation to stand up against intrusive government, *liberalism* can limit the weaknesses that come from an over reliance on leaders, even as the republican ideal can soften the excesses of too much individualism. In short, those who vocally protested the Vietnam War provided as much service to the nation as those who willingly obeyed their leaders. As Tocqueville further argued:

> It really is difficult to imagine how people who have entirely given up managing their own affairs could make a wise choice of those who are to do that for them. One should never expect a liberal, energetic, and wise government to originate in the votes of a people of servants.[32]

The challenge Americans face, then, is to retain both the faith in paternalistic leadership and the ideal of individual responsibility. Americans must champion protest and open disclosure, as well as a leader's need for secrecy and respect. In other words, America needs to treasure both the right to burn the U.S.

---

[32] ibid. p. 694.

flag in protest, and the ability to demand respect for our nation's highest symbols. American political mythology allows for this. By clinging to contradicting ideals, Americans can celebrate protest even as they celebrate obedience.

The place where the conflict between these two mythologies comes to its official head is the U.S. Supreme Court. When this happens, the Court must be careful to attempt to preserve them both. But this is the topic of Chapter Five. We must now turn to yet another element of the republican ideal that is in direct conflict with *liberalism*.

Republicanism and The Myth of The Public Good

In Chapter One, I argued that the *liberal* theory informing the Declaration of Independence expects government primarily to promote individual rights. Moreover, by assuming a state of nature where individuals enjoyed unalienable rights, *liberal* mythology fails to comprehend the notion of a public good. At most, *liberal* theory suggests that government should pursue the will of the majority of individuals in a particular society, and equates the aggregate of individual interests with the public. This way of thinking not only abounds in American political culture, but has also pervaded the study of American politics in political science departments around the country, as reflected in the dominant school of thought called pluralism.

Pluralist theory openly rejects the notion of a public interest, arguing that at most, there are groups of individuals with common special interests, but that there is no real public interest per se. For these scholars, a democratic society is one that allows all interest groups to compete fairly to determine government policy, and the public interest is no more than a compromise of the many competing special interests. According to pluralist theory, even broad concepts such as national security are ultimately matters of special interest group compromise. Though all might agree that the nation needs to be safe, the amount of money spent on security as well as what kinds of programs are pursued, is in reality determined by the competition of interest groups. In short, pluralist theory is pure Lockean *liberal* theory—it reduces all politics to the level of individual interest.

Indeed, much of American political culture conforms to this view. Special interest groups are encouraged to lobby members of Congress and the executive branch, both openly and in secret, and are allowed to donate large amounts of money to political campaigns, making it difficult to get elected without the support of numerous special interests. And finally, special interest groups, with their armies of lawyers, are always present in the halls of government agencies that iron out the actual details of broad congressional legislation. Nevertheless, this is only part of the picture. Come election time, no politician wants to be perceived as beholden to special interest groups, suggesting the presence of a completely different ideal in American political culture.

As we have seen, the republican side of American political mythology soundly rejects the argument that the purpose of government is to promote private interests, seeing government's primary responsibility instead as promoting a public interest in direct conflict with special interests. The very concepts of patriotism, leadership, and virtue discussed above, assume a public good grander than the calculated compromises of petty individual interests. From this view, a virtuous leader rises above the concerns of the individual, and a patriot sacrifices self for the good of country. Indeed, successful politicians know that this kind of ideal often proves a stronger motivator than simple economic considerations. Americans are much more willing to risk life for God and country than for oil, for example, even though oil might be an important side benefit.

As discussed in earlier chapters, the concept of the People (with its capital P) in both the Declaration and Preamble is more consistent with the republican ideal than with *liberalism*. In these primary documents, "the People" means something far greater than the compromises of competing special interests. Furthermore, only the republican ideal allows American political culture to celebrate the Declaration's signers as heroes. Because they acted for a cause higher than their individual interests, they are "founding fathers," not infamous thugs disloyal to British law and order. The Boston Tea Party is similarly colored by the republican ideal. Under the influence of *liberal* mythology, Americans would demand that individuals who destroy private property belong in prison, but the Boston Tea Party is acceptable because it led to the "birth of a nation."

Moreover, American founder James Madison was no pluralist. In *Federalist No. 10*, rather than equating the public good as the compromise between competing interest groups, as modern pluralists do, Madison argued that a large number of competing interest groups ("factions") might cancel each other out, thereby reducing their influence and allowing the public good to prevail.

Unlike in *liberal* theory, then, in republican mythology government exists to promote a cause greater than the aggregation of individual rights and interests. Yet in practice, the republican concept of the public good is difficult to define, and as John Dewey argued, the public faces a profound challenge to organize itself and make clear demands on government officials.[33] This lack of a clear public voice means that in practice, government is nearly always overwhelmed by *liberal* voices. Special interests are everywhere. Yet there remains a sense that government officials who cater too much to special interests are not living up to their public duty, suggesting that the myth of a public interest is still working to temper the excesses of individualism.

Again, I want to insist that the existence of these two contradictory mythologies constitute a great strength of American politics and not a weakness. Though pursuing the public good can be superior to pursuing petty individual interests, history is filled with stories of individuals who have suffered greatly in the name of questionable public causes, making *liberalism's* check on republicanism vital. For example, after the Japanese bombed Pearl Harbor, many loyal American citizens of Japanese descent were herded into concentration

---

[33] John Dewey, *The Public and Its Problems.*

camps without a trial and without being charged of criminal behavior. The republican ideal, with its patriotic concern for national security justified this action. And though sometimes government must, arguable, violate the self-evident, unalienable rights of many of its citizens, the *liberal* ideal makes it much more difficult to do so unnecessarily. On the other hand, excessive emphasis on individual rights leads to shortsighted policies that often pit Americans against each other with no concern for the public good. Because we need both self-sacrificing public service and self-interested resistance to unjust government power, both ideals must be preserved.

Republicanism and The Myth of The Rule of Law

Where *liberal* myth stands for popular sovereignty and control of government through separation of powers and other processes, republicanism stands for "a government of laws, not of men." This ideal rejects the concept of majority rule, because majorities can act counter to the good of society. In its pure sense, the republican ideal lacks faith in separation of powers and federalism, believing that under these practices, government officials can still act unjustly. In other words, where *liberalism* puts its faith in *processes*, (majority rule, federalism, or separation of powers), the republican myth puts its faith in *law*. The main body of the Constitution embodies a *liberal* emphasis on government processes; the Bill of Rights is more representative of the republican ideal, because it suggests that no matter what the process, there are certain things that government simply must not do, and that law guarantees this.

In actual practice, the two ideals can look somewhat similar. In fact, to the degree that the Constitution requires separation of powers, majority rule and other processes, the rule of law operates even in *liberal* theory. Nevertheless, at least in theory, the republican rule of law mythology differs significantly from *liberalism*, because it makes distinctly different demands. Where *liberal* theory allows for humans to make law, including the Constitution, the pure rule of law myth demands that law remains altogether outside human control—for where people can make and manipulate law, there exists a government of "men" and not of law.

In one way, Lockean *liberalism* seems consistent with republicanism, insofar as it posits an irrevocable natural law that stands above all human activity. And, as was argued in the previous chapter, *liberal* theory believes that all legitimate government fell within the bounds of natural law. However, in practice, *liberalism* trusts that majority rule and other processes would yield results consistent with natural law. Here republicanism and *liberalism* part ways. To be sure, *liberal* theory views the rule of law as a lofty ideal, but an ideal that is virtually unattainable due to the human proclivity towards self-bias. Consequently, *liberal* myth demands that government be organized with checks and balances to limit the damage any particular individual might do. Republican myth, however, remains committed to the ideal of the rule of law, and generally looks to virtuous leaders to uphold it.

In short, the republican rule of law ideal assumes that virtuous leaders must be the keepers of the law. American political culture thus expects public officials to rise above the culture's own pervasive *liberal* individualism and behave with public minded unselfishness. In other words, where *liberal* theory expects leaders to make laws that promote individual interests—including their own and those that got them elected, republican myth demands that leaders promote the public good, without using their positions to help particular individuals, *especially* themselves and their political supporters. Furthermore, while the republican ideal calls for a certain amount of paternalism, it demands that government officials act within the bounds of law, not as if they were laws unto themselves. This expectation is further complicated by the notion of virtue discussed above, for the virtuous leader must sometimes disregard written law in order to serve the higher principles of public good. This was certainly the logic of those signing the Declaration of Independence.

Clearly these expectations are difficult to meet, partially due to the strong demands of *liberal* theory that require public officials, at the very least, to serve the individual interests of those responsible for their election. And furthermore, it is difficult to follow a higher law without appearing to be paternalistic and out of touch with the will of the people. Once again, *liberal* mythology fundamentally opposes the republican ideal. Yet, even in the absence of *liberalism*, it would be difficult for leaders to meet the demands of republican myth on its own terms, for what might appear the virtuous path to one individual may seem entirely wrongheaded to another, and it is quite easy to view an assertive leader as acting above all law rather than in conjunction with any higher one.

The rule of law ideal makes other problematic demands. For one thing, it requires clear and easily understood laws, exact and not easily manipulated to suit individual purposes. It is difficult to make someone accountable to law if the law is unclear or overly flexible. A vague law is subject to interpretation, either by the enforcing official or by a judicial body, and whenever there is room for interpretation, the interpreter ultimately makes the law. Interpretations can change from person to person, resulting in inconsistent understandings of what the law requires. This makes a sham out of the rule of law and transfers power witty lawyers and enforcing government officials.

Ironically, many attempts to meet the demands of clarity and precision have resulted in their exact opposites—generating pages of fine print that is difficult for trained attorneys to agree upon, let alone the average citizen. Lawyers adept at finding loopholes in these laws constantly subject the reams of details to manipulation for individual ends, creating a pathetic mockery of the rule of law. The absurdity of the level of machinations that take place in the legal world was brought front and center with President Clinton's infamous questioning of the meaning of the word "is" during the sex scandal that shook his presidency. Though his statement appalled many of his critics, the legal world often turns on such questions. What starts out as the rule of law ends up being the rule of the most shrewd and resourceful.

Nor are the difficult demands of the rule of law diminished by turning to the courts for interpretation. The symbol of Lady Justice, blindfolded, and holding a set of scales, suggests a commitment to the rule of law without bias or consideration for personalities involved. The ideal demands that courts be consistent and deliberative, relying on clear standards and rendering decisions as precise and objective as the common bathroom scale. The courts, however, face a most difficult challenge living up to this ideal. The vagueness of the law that courts are asked to rule on puts them in the same realm as the lawyers. Judges too must interpret fine print and attempt to decipher meaning where meaning is vague and not self-evident. Furthermore, legislative statutes do not always capture the rule of law that the republican ideal stands for. Indeed, at times the republican myth actually requires law to be vague in order to allow judges individual discretion—assuming that particular circumstances need to be considered for justice to prevail. Where Lady Justice requires judges to be nonbiased with regard to personalities, the individual who breaks the speed limit in an attempt to save a life requires a different consideration from the one who is simply testing a new engine.

In short, the rule of law myth ultimately appeals to a concept of justice that transcends obedience to government legislation. Under *liberalism's* separation of powers scheme, the legislature must make law and the court must insure that the executive enforces what the legislature passed. However, the republican ideal, which values virtue, paternalism, and the public good, locates justice not in governmental statutes, but in the supposedly self-evident truths of a higher law, and judges are sometimes expected to operate in this realm. Where statutory law seems to run afoul of this higher form of justice, a virtuous judge will make all possible attempts to rise above it.

Nor does American political culture limit appeal to this higher law entirely to paternalistic, virtuous judges. The right to a trial by a jury of one's peers also reflects a commitment to this myth. In a jury trial, the verdict rendered by the jury is final, even if it ignores statutory law, suggesting that statutory law can be too restrictive or too myopic to result in true justice. Indeed the right to a trial by a jury of one's peers suggests a commitment to a higher law that requires a deeply intimate understanding of the individual in question.

Yet such highly specific justice is extremely problematic and vulnerable to criticism. A justice so dependent on unique circumstances prevents anyone other than those directly involved from fully understanding the thinking behind it, so that what might seem like justice to those handing it out may appear a sham to those looking on. Such was the case following the trials of O.J. Simpson and the police officers charged with the unlawful beating of Rodney King, in which many felt justice had been bought rather than served. And significantly, there is no way to prove otherwise. When those exercising power do attempt to meet the demands of republican mythology, they are most vulnerable.

The challenge to preserve the rule of law becomes even more complex when courts are called on to settle constitutional questions. As will be shown, the republican ideal ultimately considers even the Constitution subject to a higher law, while it also considers the Constitution a higher law than statutes passed by typical legislative bodies. Consequently, legislative acts that violate the Constitution are considered unlawful. Yet to determine that a legislative act is unconstitutional requires some entity or institution to take the initiative on the matter, and when the Supreme Court does this, the rule of law itself is jeopardized.

Recall that the founders refused to openly grant the Supreme Court the power to determine an act of Congress unconstitutional, because to do so would grant the Supreme Court too much legislative power (see Chapter Two). As a result, whenever the Court does exercise this power, its legitimacy will always come under question. Not only does the Court violate the separation of powers myth, it also potentially violates the rule of law ideal, as no law grants the Court this power. What happens when the Court gets it wrong? What law prevails then?

The Court has adopted two strategies to avoid the perception that something is wrong when it rules on the constitutionality of an act of Congress. First, justices generally root their decisions in the language of the Constitution and precedent cases, thus suggesting that the Court itself does not make law, but relies on the intent of those who wrote the Constitution or the precedents handed down from prior cases. Secondly, the Court relies on the republican ideal which looks to virtuous individuals to uphold the rule of law. Where *liberal* theory relies on the ability of others to check the actions of those in power, the republican ideal perceives a need for virtuous individuals to operate without excessive oversight. This ideal justifies life terms for Court members and gives the Supreme Court final say in questions of constitutionality. Free from the petty political concerns of most politicians, justices can be best relied on to insure the rule of law.

Nevertheless, since the Constitution does not clearly grant this power to the Court, and since precedent cases can be variously interpreted, the legitimacy of Court rulings, not to mention the virtue of the justices, is seldom accepted to all parties concerned. Their decisions are always vulnerable to the perception that the rule of law has been replaced by the rule of the majority of politically appointed justices. Paradoxically, the rule of law myth demands that the Court both exercise and refrain from exercising final say over Congress.

This most capricious myth becomes even more problematic by subjecting the Constitution itself to a higher law. For example, though the practice of slavery was intentionally protected by the Constitution, and though it was illegal to help runaway slaves, American political culture today celebrates the heroic actions of those who illegally helped and encouraged runaways. In fact, it could be argued that in the most infamous Supreme Court decision ever handed down, the *Dred Scott* case, the Court shrunk from its duty even while wrapping its decision in the Constitution. In *Dred Scott,* the Court argued that, unjust as it might seem, the Constitution did not grant citizenship to freed slaves and there was nothing the Court or Congress could do about it, short of amending the Constitution.

In sum, the rule of law ideal creates a difficult, if not disturbing, catch-22 for all involved, especially the Supreme Court. The ideal assumes a law that is meant to govern the human experience and transcend human manipulation—a mythical ideal if there ever was one, as it is impossible to enforce a law lying outside the human experience without tainting it with human hands. Nevertheless, the ideal of the rule of law rightly remains an integral part of American political culture. As impossible as it may be to practice, we still look to it to protect us from the excesses of the democratic process. The Bill of Rights remains a key symbol of American freedom.

Conclusion

Republicanism, then, enriches American political culture in ways quite contrary to those of classic *liberal* theory. Planting its faith in the rule of law, republicanism distrusts the *liberal* reliance on processes and checks and balances. It finds the *liberal* emphasis on individual rights too narrow and self-indulgent, and endeavors to use government to promote the public good, even, sometimes, at the expense of the individual. And finally, the republican ideal, while embracing paternalism, demands virtuous leaders, something that *liberal* theory considers highly improbable and thus foolhardy to expect. Arguably, where *liberalism's* primary emphasis on individual rights constantly questions the legitimacy of government initiatives and thus consistently threatens to pull society apart, republicanism provides American political culture a balancing impulse toward unification.

America is a tremendously diverse nation; significant cultural, ethnic, religious, and economic differences constantly threaten to divide it. All Americans really share little if anything concrete in common. Given this, patriotism, flag waving, and Fourth of July celebrations where American heroes committed to the selfless ideals of republicanism are visibly extolled, are indispensable to a strong, united nation. Moreover, the republican expectation that individuals in power serve the public, as opposed to their personal narrow interests, provides a vital check on extreme individualism. The rule of law tempers what could be mob-rule democracy. On the other hand, the republican ideal's anti-democratic paternalism leaves its position in American politics precarious. As suggested above, virtuous acts are not that clear to everyone concerned, and the American *liberal* heritage looks towards republicanism with a skeptical eye.

This skepticism is well founded. In the past, "virtuous" men, acting in the name of the public good, have promoted some highly questionable practices, including slavery and the treatment of women as second-class citizens. Indeed, it could be argued that as America has become more committed to *liberalism*, more individuals have enjoyed the unalienable rights enshrined in the Declaration of Independence.

Yet *liberal* theory in its extreme form still threatens to pull the nation apart, giving rise to angry resentful radio commentators such as Rush Limbaugh, and a growing number of committed "libertarians" who view most government initiatives as "socialistic" and violations of individual liberties. Extreme *liberal* individualism champions gun rights and a growing number of fanatic anti-government militia groups. Nor has their criticism been limited to abstract theory, as the nation discovered on April 19, 1995, when Timothy McVeigh blew up the Oklahoma City federal building. These individuals and groups see themselves as true patriots rooted in the logic of Thomas Jefferson and unalienable individual rights.

Ironically, then, one of the biggest threats to the republican ideal comes from the activist core of the Republican Party itself. The Republican emphasis on free-trade capitalism, individual property rights, and small government with a very limited public role directly opposes the republican ideal. So does the Republican cry for mandatory sentencing of drug offenders and other criminals, suggesting as it does a lack of faith in a judge's virtue.

But Democrats are also highly critical of elements of republicanism. Though often guilty of paternalism themselves, Democratic activists consistently speak out against anything that smacks of elitist paternalism as they work for more democratic processes. Furthermore, Democrats work hard for equal rights for women and minorities, and promote freedom of individual expression in art, culture, and sexuality.

In short, republican ideals are and always have been under constant attack from all sides in American politics. This does not mean that they are necessarily in any immediate danger of going away. The same Democrats and Republicans who criticize republican ideals also support them. Many in both parties speak openly about the need to restore virtue and public service. Democrats and Republicans alike extol the virtue of the rule of law and are hardly bashful about asking government to promote the public good. However, this does not mean that care should not be taken to insure the survival of this ideal.

Perhaps the greatest threat to the republican myth emerges when those entrusted with governmental power seem blatantly to ignore republicanism's high demands. When elites obviously use their power to promote personal agendas, Jeffersonian *liberalism* is most strongly felt and the public demands more democracy. The cry for term limits, for example, came about when distrust of government officials, perceived as laws unto themselves, out of touch with their constituencies, reached critical mass. Calls for mandatory sentencing determined by legislatures reflect a perception that judges have political agendas that interfere with their duty to insure justice. And calls for judicial restraint reflect a perception that paternalistic judges make policy to promote their own positions rather than uphold the law.

Again, the U.S. Supreme Court has a most important role in preserving the republican ideal; in fact, I argue that this is the Court's most natural realm. The Court deals in law, justices are appointed for life in order to be isolated from regular political processes, and the symbolism and secrecy of Court deliberations promotes the ideal of wise men and women carefully weighing the facts away from the raucous demands of democratic politics. Generally, the justices take this role very seriously. They are careful to write opinions grounded in the Constitution and formerly established precedent. For example, note the words of Justice Anthony Kennedy as he sided with the majority in ruling that the Constitution assures a right to burn the American flag in protest:

> [S]ometimes we must make decisions we do not like. We make them because they are right, right in the sense that the law and the Constitution, as we see them, compel the result. And so great is our commitment to the process that, except in the rare case, we do not pause to express distaste for the result, perhaps for fear of undermining a valued principle that dictates the decision.[34]

In fact, the Court's commitment to the republican ideal perhaps best explains its prestigious place in American politics. *Liberal* distrust of politicians ("men are not angels") creates a built-in suspicion of presidents and members of Congress. Supreme Court justices, on the other hand, are generally looked at through the lenses of the republican ideal. Only when the Court seems to openly stray from its republican obligations does it attract widespread criticism.

Such was the case in the *Bush* v. *Gore* 2000 presidential election case. To those critical of the Court, it appeared that the justices in the majority blatantly abandoned their commitment to the rule of law and become nothing more than super politicians, willing to use their powerful positions to promote political self-interest. Many articles in newspapers, news magazines, and scholarly journals,

---

[34] *Texas v. Johnson* 491 U.S. 397 1989.

openly accused the Court in these terms. And it was this perception that upset the critics most, so they claimed, and not the Court's ruling in favor of a particular candidate. Determining the accuracy of this claim is not the purpose of this chapter. Obviously, Gore supporters were bound to be disappointed by the Court's ruling and the fact that Gore supporters tended to be more distraught with the Court for abandoning its role than Bush supporters indicates that a degree of partisanship influenced their perceptions. Nevertheless, the torrent of criticism that followed the decision indicates that the Court is most vulnerable when it appears to stray from its obligation to uphold and live up to the republican ideals.

That said, as much as the Court's critics may hate to admit it, the justices in the *Bush* v. *Gore* case, were arguably attempting to live up to the demands of the republican ideal. To be sure, all five of the majority justices reversed their own precedents and established jurisprudence, which they consistently and regularly followed before *Bush* v. *Gore*, and went back to following after that case. Furthermore, all five of the majority justices clearly had strong personal preferences for the Republican candidate, making their decision to abandon their own established jurisprudence to insure the election of George W. Bush seem all the more dubious.[35] Nevertheless, the republican ideal ultimately demands leaders to sacrifice even their own reputations, if that is what is required for the good of the nation. It could be argued that this is exactly what happened in this situation: all five justices, knowing that by reversing their established principles they would appear not only hypocritically but also in violation of their judicial oaths, were nevertheless willing to pay this price for the good of the nation.[36]

Moreover, the fact that numerous individuals were not upset by the Court's actions in the 2000 presidential election may suggest that the majority

---

[35] For a detailed and convincing argument of this, see Alan Dershowitz, *Supreme Injustice: How the High Court Hijacked Election 2000.*

[36] If this were the case, it would be most Machiavellian indeed. Obviously we will never know for sure what the motives of these justices were. And this is one of the more difficult demands of the republican ideal. Virtue is not always evident, and those who exercise it may seem to all others as paternalistic and selfishly political.

succeeded in living up to the demands of republican virtue. Indeed, most Americans have no idea how completely the Court abandoned its own jurisprudential principles to get this result. Most Americans do not pay enough attention to the Court to make this type of judgment. Court supporters perceived it as acting in its most typical republican role, as having the final responsibility to get it right, and in this case, to save the nation from the endless squabbling endemic to democratic politics. In the eyes of many Bush supporters, this is what the Court did. In one quick ruling the Court ended the matter once and for all and gave the nation the proper president.

In his book *Supreme Injustice*, Alan Dershowitz challenges the argument that the Court's actions in *Bush* v. *Gore* should be judged by the success or failure of the Bush presidency.[37] As a Harvard law professor, Dershowitz wants to hold the Court accountable for its actions on their own merits and argues that this should have nothing to do with the outcome. For him, what the Court did in *Bush* v. *Gore* was wrong simply because they failed to live up to their judicial oaths. In his words, they "virtually placed *themselves* above the law, not only by rendering this lawless decision, but by refusing to be bound by the same rules of judicial conduct that govern all other judges."[38] These five justices may very well be guilty as charged. Nevertheless, American political culture is not concerned with such technicalities and, Dershowitz's claim notwithstanding, will judge the Court's actions by the success of the Bush presidency, just as it has judged the actions of the Boston Tea Party members by their success, and just as it has judged the actions of those who signed the Declaration of Independence by their success. American political culture tells the story of the nation; it seldom burdens itself with the technical legal arguments of constitutional law scholars.

Nevertheless, the relationship between scholars, governing elites, and American political culture is complex, and over time, the actions of the Court in

---

[37] Dershowitz, p. 177.
[38] Ibid., p. 179.

Bush v. *Gore* may very well result in negative repercussions not limited to the success or failure of the Bush presidency. Elites entrusted with the strings of power in American politics are very much aware that the five justices in the majority in *Bush* v. *Gore* violated their own established jurisprudential principles, and acted outside of the typical rule of law demands of the Court in order to insure a Republican victory. Some of these elites will undoubtedly view the Court as having acted in its higher republican role, as having risen above written law and personal jurisprudence in order to promote the higher law of national preservation. But others are bound to retain the cynical view that with its actions in *Bush* v. *Gore*, the justices lowered themselves to the level of power politicians and in doing so, greatly harmed the prestige of the Court.[39] If the day ever comes, when the nation looks to *Bush* v. *Gore* as a major step towards elites themselves becoming cynical to the point of losing faith in the republican myth of virtue altogether, it could prove to be a most unfortunate decision. The health of the republican ideal lies ultimately in the hands of the elites. When they stop thinking of it as a legitimate ideal, America may indeed suffer from an onslaught of unchecked *liberal* individualism and "democratic distemper."[40]

---

[39] Similar to the way Judge Bork views many actions of the Court in the past. See his book, *The Tempting of America*.

[40] See Samuel Huntington's, *Democratic Distemper*, found in Paul Schumaker, Dwight C. Kiel, and Thomas W. Heilke, eds., *Ideological Voices: An Anthology in Modern Political Ideas* (New York: The McGraw-Hill Companies, Inc. 1997), p. 277.

Supreme Justice

Chapter Four
The Inadequacies of Judicial Philosophies

Debate over the proper role of the Supreme Court in American politics continues to challenge Court watchers both in academic and public forums. Awareness of this debate reached new heights with the Court's actions in the controversial 2000 presidential election contest. And though the particulars differ from case to case, the issue is always the same: when does the Court overstep its boundaries by entering either of the two forbidden realms: the realm of state jurisdiction or the realm of law making?

As indicated in the first three chapters, this controversy resists resolution largely because of the richly contradictory mythical ideals of American political culture. Due to its paradoxical position, the Supreme Court receives strong but mixed messages from American political mythology. Consistently told that it is a judicial body with limited judicial functions, the Court is also expected to play a much bigger political role, a role unlike that of any other political entity. To fully grasp this argument, a brief analysis of the term *politics* and American political culture's understanding of this term is in order.

In *liberal* mythology, "politics" has a largely negative connotation. *Liberalism* envisions a body of self-evident universal truths that predate government and are not open to debate, manipulation, or compromise. *Liberalism* thus sees no real need for politics. Politics becomes the dirty business of crafty, if not outright dishonest, politicians whose secret manipulations and compromises promote their own and other's special interests at the expense of truth. *Liberal* mythology sees all of this as not only unnecessary but morally wrong. Truth need never be hidden, manipulated or compromised over.

This rejection of politics has not always been the norm. Aristotle, for example, viewed the political practice of determining which values a society must enforce as one of the highest possible human endeavors. Aristotle understood society as consisting of many individuals with many different and often conflicting values. Politics, for Aristotle, was the difficult practice of finding a balance that all could live with and that would allow society to flourish.

In his 1790 *Reflections on the Revolution in France,* Edmund Burke provided an Aristotelian critique of the emerging *liberal* theory of government. Like Aristotle, Burke argued that political leaders had historically understood questions of liberty and justice as complex social matters. Burke also assumed the existence of conflicting and competing values in any society, and believed that only a mixture of these values could be enforced by government institutions. Politics, he believed, was the process that determined what the proper mix would be. In short, determining political justice, Burke argued, was an intricate and multifarious task, requiring endless compromise, evaluation, and balance. Burke consequently viewed the new *liberal* doctrine of self-evident natural rights as an overly simplistic view of social reality.[41]

This chapter concerns not whether Burke was correct but what he implies about the American understanding of politics. For in a sense, *liberal* theory rejects the need for traditional politics altogether. Because the self-evident natural law predetermines a society's legitimate values, no government institution should be necessary to determine those values. Social justice, equally pre-determined by natural law, is considered self-evident to all honest, decent citizens.

Although few Supreme Court justices will ever openly state it, and Supreme Court scholars consistently avoid acknowledging or even contemplating

---

[41] Edmund Burke, *Reflections on the Revolution in France*, found in Paul Schumaker, Dwight C. Kiel, and Thomas W. Heilke, eds. *Ideological Voices: An Anthology in Modern Political Ideas* (New York: The McGraw-Hill Companies Inc. 1997).

it, American political culture actually requires the Supreme Court to uphold and preserve this self-evident natural law. This requirement happens more by default than design, because the Court is expected to *interpret* the Constitution. If the Constitution were crystal clear, it would only have to be *applied.* Since the Court must interpret it, the Court must give it meaning. And American political mythology demands that the meaning the Court gives the Constitution is consistent with self-evident natural law.

This understanding does little to resolve the question, though it does help explain the eternal controversy over the Court's proper role. A self-evident natural law needs no interpretation; in practice, however, interpreting the Constitution through the lens of natural law requires the Court to be very political. That is, by determining what is constitutional, the Court by default engages in the traditional political role of determining what values American society will enforce. American political culture grants this role to no other government institution; *liberal* theory, committed to self-evident natural law, grants it to no institution at all.

Given this, the Court constantly finds itself in impossible situations. The very fact that cases demanding constitutional interpretation come to the Supreme Court suggests that the proper interpretation of the Constitution is not always self-evident. Consequently, no matter how it rules, the Court's interpretations will never be self-evident either. This is why unanimous decisions are so important to the Court, particularly in highly politicized, controversial cases. A 5-4 ruling, hardly suggests a self-evident Constitution.

In short, America's mythological rejection of politics ultimately underlies the controversy over the Court's proper role in American politics. The Constitution, understood as requiring state governments as well as Congress to abide by the self-evident truths of natural law, is also expected to reflect these self-evident truths, which the Supreme Court duly interprets. But because no government institution has the authority to violate this natural law, and natural law is not open to debate and manipulation, the Supreme Court cannot help but be perceived by someone as tampering with natural law every time it rules on the constitutionality of state or national government action. This is the fundamental source of the nation's inability to agree on the Court's proper role.

Moreover, the vagueness of the concept of natural law is difficult to deal with practically. Though its mythological demands cannot be ignored, to meaningfully implement natural law is difficult, if not impossible. Mythological, self-evident natural rights provide little guidance for the day-to-day challenges of governing. Consequently, most debate over the proper role of the Supreme Court understandably focuses on more concrete principles: separation of powers, majority rule, the rule of law, and checks and balances.

As described in Chapter Two, the separation of powers ideal envisions the power to determine what values a society will enforce by law as a legislative power—the power to make law. Thus the judicial function, in its pure sense, is strictly limited to insuring that executive officials enforce the law fairly and impartially. Though a judge must interpret law in order to decide whether executive officials are enforcing it impartially, the actual interpreting of the law is not the judicial function per se, but only a preliminary requirement. In fact, had the legislative body drafted sufficiently clear laws, no judicial interpretation would be needed.

It was further argued in Chapter Two that the separation of powers ideal does not consider declaring an act of Congress unconstitutional part of the judicial function. Though examining an act of Congress to determine its constitutionality is known as *judicial review*, it is nevertheless not a traditional judicial power. Judicial review is ultimately a legislative power, as it is the power to determine the law.

Court oversight of Congress, to insure that its legislation is constitutional, was thus not part of the checks and balances process the founders put in place, for such a direct grant of power to the Supreme Court would seriously compromise the separation of powers principle.

Significantly, then, when the Court exercises the power of judicial review, it is considered legitimate only in so far as its decision does not *appear* as a legislative action. But since the Court clearly *is* making law in exercising this power, it can hardly appear otherwise. And because separation of powers theory demands that the Court refrain from making law, constitutional scholars, politicians, judges, and justices alike, have all attempted to explain when and how the Court can legitimately get involved in this obvious political activity. Although, there has been little agreement, no one in the mainstream of American political discourse argues that the Court should refrain from using this power altogether. All seem to sense that it must.

In this chapter, we examine the prevailing arguments about when and why the Court should exercise the power of judicial review. All are fundamentally flawed and hence inadequate, because all fail to fully comprehend the highly political demands American mythology makes on the Court. None of the major theories appreciate the richness of American political culture and the inherent importance of its mythical idealism.

Judicial Restraint Theories

Many who consider themselves "conservatives" adhere to a philosophy of judicial restraint, which theoretically pays strict attention to the separation of powers principle and argues that the Court does not have the responsibility to make law. Many such conservatives are a bit confused, however, when they argue that the Court's job is to "*interpret* and not *make* law." They fail to understand that the power to interpret law is the power to make law. Nevertheless, they consistently advocate a limited, conservative role for the Court in American politics; that is, the Court should not initiate new governmental protections, rather it should adhere to the tried and true.

Conservatives tend to view the Court of the 1950s through early 1970s as "activist" in so far as it often led the way towards social change during that period. In 1954, for example, the Court ruled that segregated schools were unconstitutional—demanding that many states change their policies for dealing with racial tensions. (*Brown* v. *Board of Education of Topeka* 347 U.S. 483, 74 S.Ct. 686, 98 L.Ed. 873 1954.) In 1964, the Court mandated the one-person-one-vote rule—forcing many states to change the way they drew up their legislative districts. (*Reynolds* v. *Sims* 377 U.S. 533, 84 S.Ct. 1362, 12 L.Ed.2d 506 1964.) And most egregiously, in 1973 the Court determined that a woman's right to choose an abortion was a protected right of the Constitution—thus overturning many state abortion laws. (*Roe* v. *Wade,* 410 U.S. 113, 93 S.Ct. 705, 35 L.Ed.2d 147 1973.) Conservatives generally feel that in these cases the Court was wrong in actively striking down laws that had been enforced for years under the umbrella of the Constitution. Furthermore, conservatives argue that even if such changes are necessary, it is the legislature's responsibility to make them and not the Supreme Court's.

Ironically, today's conservatives are shortsighted in calling for judicial restraint as theories of judicial restraint are necessarily conservative. It is conservative to encourage the Court to uphold traditions, but deference to a democratically elected legislature is not necessarily a conservative ideal. In Chapter Three, for example, it was shown that American political culture has traditionally embraced elitist republican values quite skeptical of the virtues of democracy. In fact, conservatives have traditionally been stubbornly resistant to the spread of democratic principles. Conservatives have, for example, favored poll taxes and literacy tests, practices clearly meant to keep certain people from participating in the democratic process. In short, it would be quite consistent with republican values to view the Court as an institution that, by virtue of the fact that it stands above the political fray, bears the clear responsibility to protect the nation from the excesses of democracy.

Nevertheless, contemporary calls for judicial restraint come largely from the so-called conservative camp, probably in reaction to the judicial activism of recent history. It is to these theories of judicial restraint that we will turn to first.

Originalism

One of the arguments for judicial restraint is the argument of original intent or originalism. Originalist Robert Bork, whose nomination to the Supreme Court by President Ronald Reagan was rejected by the Senate, roots his argument for judicial restraint in the separation of powers ideal, the theory of democracy, and the rule of law.[42] He reasons that the Court should generally defer to Congress, since the Constitution explicitly grants Congress all legislative power to make law, and since the theory of majority rule demands that those individuals elected by the people to make law do so. For Bork, allowing the non-elected Supreme Court to make law violates fundamental principles of the Constitution.

Bork further argues that the rule of law principle demands that the Court simply uphold the law, whether it likes it or not. To be sure, in order to be consistent, Bork would have to argue that the Court should avoid the exercise of judicial review altogether, since it is not explicitly granted in the Constitution. Yet Bork is not a pure theorist. As an active player in American politics, he promotes a pragmatic judicial philosophy suited to political reality, where the Court's power to exercise judicial review is not in question. Consequently, Bork, and all judicial restraint advocates must and do accept the Court's judicial review power. However, Bork argues that this power must be restrained as much as possible. Otherwise, he reasons, instead of majority rule or the rule of law, the nation would be subjected to the despotic rule of the justices sitting on the Supreme Court.

[42] See Robert H. Bork, *The Original Understanding* found in Susan J. Brison and Walter Sinnott-Armstrong, eds., *Contemporary Perspectives on Constitutional Interpretation* (Boulder: Westview Press 1993).

For Bork, the best way to insure that the justices' personal agendas do not interfere with their judgment is to require them to abide by the original intent of those who wrote the law. In his judgment, the practice of seeking original intent both pays homage to the demands of the separation of powers principle, and also supports the rule of law ideal. Supreme Court Justice Antonin Scalia similarly argues that if one is going to rely on the Constitution to determine the legitimacy of an act of Congress at all, one must assume that the Constitution has an original meaning.[43] This original meaning must be sought out and followed. Otherwise, it is argued, we fail to rely on the Constitution as the paramount law. If the Constitution is not considered to have any original meaning, it is absurd to look to it as the source of law. In other words, Justice Scalia argues, if the Constitution can mean anything, it provides no standard whatsoever, and there is no reason to use it. Moreover, originalists argue that as long as Court justices attempt to follow the reasoning of those who made the law, they can minimize the influence of their own personal agendas, thus preserving the principle of separation of powers and the rule of law.

This argument is quite compelling at first blush. As long as justices follow the drafters' intentions, they cannot insert their own political agendas and jeopardize the rule of law. In practice, it proves to be quite problematic, and criticism of this position abounds. Much of this criticism has been thoroughly made elsewhere and there is no need to reiterate it here. But it must be noted that *decisively* determining a single unified intent of those who wrote the Constitution has proven impossible, and therefore demanding that justices rely on the original intent ultimately resolves nothing. Even if every single Court justice agreed that following original intent was imperative, there would be serious and interminable disagreement over what that intent was.

For example, it is difficult, if not impossible, to know the original intent of the founders' prohibition of "cruel and unusual punishment." Why did they leave

---

[43] See Antonin Scalia, *Originalism: The Lesser Evil*, 57 U.Cinn.L.Rev. 849 (1989).

this phrase so vague? Did they intend to make the Constitution flexible from one generation to another, or to legitimize permanently the practices of their time? Such questions are agonizingly difficult to answer, as Bork's own illustrations show. For example, he argues that since capital punishment was allowed in early American history, the words "cruel and unusual" could not possibly refer to the death penalty today.[44] Nevertheless, Bork also denies that slavery was perpetually protected by the Constitution just because it was allowed in the original understanding of the document.[45] How Bork reaches these contradictory positions is mystifying. Discovering whether or not the founders intended for capital punishment to be guaranteed throughout American history would be a difficult task, and even though the word *slavery* never explicitly appears in the Constitution, Bork is forced to ignore certain key phrases as well as a giant block of history, including a Civil War, to reach his conclusion.

More damaging, however, to the originalist position, is the fact that few of its adherents are willing to fully practice it. Justice Scalia, for example, sees himself as a "fainthearted" originalist, believing it wrong to uphold a state practice of public lashing or branding of the right hand, though the founders made no laws against such punishments.

But perhaps what is most problematic with originalism is its failure to provide meaningful guidance. Justice Scalia himself argues that sometimes the original intent of the founders should not be followed. Furthermore, a consistent theory of judicial restraint would require that justices never exercise the power of judicial review. Since advocates of judicial restraint are unwilling to go this far, they are compelled to explain when restraint should and should not be followed; hence their theory is ultimately dependent on some other theory. These theorists generally argue that the Court must proceed when acts of Congress are clearly in violation to the Constitution as understood by the original intent of the founders.

---

[44] Robert H. Bork, *The Tempting of America: The Political Seduction of the Law*, p. 214.
[45] Ibid., pp. 28-34.

This is no help, as few would argue that the Court should overturn a clearly constitutional act of Congress. The debate is simply shifted to the question of when is a Congressional act in clear violation of the original intent of the founders. And inevitably, personal opinion, the very thing originalists want to avoid, becomes the only thing justices can rely on.

The originalist theory of judicial restraint also fails to guide justices in dealing with difficult precedent cases. Generally, justices feel compelled to base their decisions on precedent, as this supports the ideal of consistent and predictable law. However, this raises a difficult dilemma for the justice who argues that the original intent of the founders should be followed. What happens when the rulings of previous justices differ from one's own understanding of original intent? Should justices follow their personal interpretation of the founder's intent, or the precedent cases in question? Bork argues that generally a justice should go with precedent, as consistency and predictability are important enough *on their own merits* to justify doing so. Presumably Bork would include those precedents establishing the Court's power to exercise judicial review as falling into this category. However, Bork also argues that sometimes precedent is so blatantly wrong for society that it should be overturned in favor of the perceived original intent. The question is, how do individual justices know when to uphold precedent and when to overturn it?

Remarkably, Bork recommends *prudence* as the final guide. When it seems prudent to go against precedent, the justice should do so.[46] This too is clearly problematic, as is evidenced by the 1992 *Planned Parenthood* v. *Casey* abortion case. In this case, the so-labeled conservative Reagan appointee Justice Sandra Day O'Conner argued that people had come to rely on the rights guaranteed by the controversial *Roe* v. *Wade* abortion case, and that therefore prudence demanded that it be upheld. Four justices agreed with her and four justices disagreed, thinking it more prudent for the Court to get out of the abortion

[46] See Robert H. Bork, *The Original Understanding.*

business altogether. Which of these justices are correct? Which are the most prudent?

Worse still, Bork's admonition that justices rely on prudence completely undermines the originalist theory. The whole point of originalism (as Bork puts it) is to keep justices from doing the very thing Bork ultimately requires them to do—use their own judgment. In short, Bork has made the demand to follow the original intent of the founders contingent on prudence, as determined by the individual justices. "Be wise," he tells the justice. "Follow your conscience." If the intent of originalists is to ban justices from relying on their own ideas of justice, this final admonition demonstrates the inadequacy of originalism.

But however much Bork's appeal to prudence undermines his own theory, it is rooted in American political culture. As argued above, the *liberal* belief in natural law virtually demands that Supreme Court justices prudently exercise judicial review to insure that government officials abide by its self-evident truths. Bork's faith in prudence echoes Jefferson's faith in self-evident truths. Indeed, today's conservatives seem to believe that what seems prudent to them is self-evident to all honest and upright American citizens. The call to prudence also harmonizes with the republican celebration of paternalism and Machiavellian virtue. Unfortunately, paternalism is inconsistent with judicial restraint, however, and Bork is ultimately telling sitting justices to be *activists* if prudence demands it.

In sum, original intent advocates like Bork contradict themselves by encouraging both prudence on the one hand and judicial restraint on the other—they fail to offer a consistent, reliable judicial theory. Though they sense that the Court must exercise the power of judicial review, they fail to comprehend the paradoxical and mythical nature of this demand, and consequently cannot provide a good justification for its use.

Framework for Democracy Theory

Other conservatives, notably the late Chief Justice William H. Rehnquist, adhere to another version of judicial restraint that strictly emphasizes the separation of powers theory and basically envisions the Constitution as the rulebook according to which a democratic society should play. The Court, from this perspective, is like society's referee. Referees do not make rules in the middle of the game. Their job is to insure that the rules previously determined are followed. Likewise, the Court must avoid making rules and restrict its actions simply to insuring that executives enforce the law according to the will of the people as reflected by their representatives in the legislature.[47] Chief Justice Rehnquist thus rejected the argument that the Supreme Court should act to right the wrongs of society. It is the legislature's responsibility, not the Court's, to determine what evils it wants to address. As he explained:

> Even in the face of a conceded social evil, a reasonably competent and reasonably representative legislature may decide to do nothing. It may decide that the evil is not of sufficient magnitude to warrant any governmental intervention. It may decide that the financial cost of eliminating the evil is not worth the benefit which would result from its elimination. It may decide that the evils which might ensue from the proposed solution are worse than the evils which the solution would eliminate. ...[48]

Accordingly, Rehnquist argued that the Court should exercise judicial review only to enforce compliance with the rules of democracy laid out in the Constitution. For him, so long as the democratic process was followed, the laws passed by a legislative body must be upheld. Only when the legislative body has acted outside of the rules can the Court declare their laws to be unconstitutional. The Court has no power to make rules itself.

---

[47] See William H. Rehnquist, *The Notion of a Living Constitution*, found in Walter F. Murphy, James E. Fleming, and Sotirios A. Barber, *American Constitutional Interpretation*, Second Edition (New York: Foundation Press, 1995).

[48] Ibid., p. 247

University of Miami law professor John Hart Ely similarly believes that the Constitution implicitly requires the Court to exercise judicial review; nevertheless, he argues, justices on the Court are in no position to determine which values a society should uphold. Justices can insure that the process for making such determinations stays open, he reasons, and this should be the primary question they ask in looking at cases.[49]

The Rehnquist/Ely argument also seems legitimate at first. It strongly supports the separation of powers principle, theoretically limiting the Court's judicial review powers to acceptable bounds and thus keeping legislative power in the legislature where it belongs. At this point in my argument, it should come as no surprise, however, that in practice, this theory also proves to be inadequate as it ignores vital elements of much American political culture.

As shown in previous chapters, American political mythology does not envision a legislature fully authorized to pass any law, even if it does follow the proper democratic process. American political culture envisions autonomous individuals enjoying God-given unalienable rights which government simply may not violate. These rights are absolute, and a government that violates them, even by majority vote, is illegitimate. Moreover, as determined in Chapter Three, American political culture endorses certain republican principles as well, and Rehnquist read the Constitution selectively when he limited it to a simple framework for democracy. The presence of the Bill of Rights alone demands a deeper reading. And the Ninth Amendment, which states that there are rights not listed in the Bill of Rights that are retained by the people, is a reminder that the founders were not at all willing to leave the rights of the people to be determined by a democratic process.

Ely has a more sophisticated argument; however, it too suffers from a limited acceptance of the demands of American political culture. Though he

[49] John Hart Ely, *Democracy and Distrust: A Theory of Judicial Review* (Cambridge: Harvard University Press, Third Printing 1980).

acknowledges that the Bill of Rights in general, and the Ninth Amendment in particular, demand that the Court exercise judicial review over Congress, he ultimately rejects these demands, convinced that justices themselves are in no position to determine what the unlisted constitutional rights might be, and sees no acceptable alternative but to put his faith in the democratic process. This is where his argument becomes inadequate. It provides no consolation to individuals who feel their God-given rights are being violated, no matter how open the process was that led to this violation. And though Ely may correctly sense that justices have no monopoly on wisdom by which to determine what rights are and are not protected by the open-ended Ninth Amendment, the founders, as stated above, were much less willing than he to trust the democratic process. In fact, the specific purpose of the Bill of Rights was to protect individuals from the processes of government the Constitution created. In short, Ely senses that various clauses in the Constitution (including the Ninth Amendment) demand that the Court exercise judicial review, yet Ely fails to comprehend the degree to which those clauses demand that the processes of the majority be kept in check. So while he rightly argues that justices as individuals have no ultimate authority, he fails to acknowledge that legislatures and majorities have no such authority either. Natural law gives this authority to no one. By granting the majority full responsibility to protect minorities, Ely trusts the fox to guard the hen house.

This reliance on the democratic process to determine America's values is an odd state of affairs for modern conservatives. As stated above, today's theories of judicial restraint grew largely out of a reaction to the aggressive actions of the Warren Court, which had a greater interest in promoting certain individual rights than did Congress and most state legislatures. (Ely first wrote his argument for restraint in 1938, and his motives should not be confused with those of contemporary conservatives.) Given the Court's promotion of abortion rights, extra protections for the accused, and forced desegregation, conservative criticism is understandable. But in choosing to champion the democratic process as a means of reining in the Court, conservatives in many ways ended up discounting, even rejecting, key elements of the traditional republican ideal in which they generally believe. In other words, it is not clear that the theory of judicial restraint and legislative deference is really a conservative position at all. To the extent that conservatives believe in wise elites practicing selfless virtue for the good of the nation, one would expect them to favor an activist Court willing to exercise authority over the results of the less contemplative democratic process. And indeed, conservatives did favor such a Court in the controversial 2000 presidential contest. Suddenly, judicial restraint conservatives looked to the Court to save the nation from its own messy democracy. And perhaps the abruptness of their deathbed repentance was equaled only by the quick conversion of liberals to the principle of judicial restraint. In his criticism of the Court's involvement in that case, liberal Harvard law professor Alan Dershowitz accused the Court of the very same undemocratic paternalism for which conservatives have so consistently criticized the Court.[50]

Theories of Judicial Activism

Many contemporary liberals, or at least those accused by others as being "liberal," subscribe to judicial philosophies that promote a more activist Supreme Court. These individuals are liberal in that they privilege the traditional *liberal* belief in unalienable and inviolable individual rights. They are liberal in the eyes of their critics because they believe that list of self-evident unalienable rights includes many that earlier generations did not find self-evident, including, the equal treatment of women, the equal treatment of all individuals regardless of sexual orientation, and the equal treatment of all individuals regardless of religious preferences or ethnicity. These individuals often grant the Supreme Court a more proactive role in insuring these rights and a responsibility to stand up against the majority will and guarantee the constitutional rights of minorities.

---

[50] See Alan M. Dershowitz, *Supreme Injustice*.

Significantly, however, so-called liberals do not see themselves as asking the Court to make law, as their critics so often charge. Liberals also believe that the Constitution needs to be followed. However, they understand the Constitution to require a Court that will right the wrongs of a majority controlled society. For them, the Constitution guarantees certain rights, and the Court must insure that majorities respect those rights.

However, it is no clearer why this is a "liberal" position than why judicial restraint is a "conservative" one. As suggested in the conclusion of the last section, today's conservatives also look to the Court to protect the nation from unruly democratic processes. Moreover, many liberals criticized the Rehnquist Court for its conservative judicial activism in striking down legislation it considered imprudent—including, for example, the affirmative action programs that suffered greatly under the Rehnquist reign. This activism became most visible when the Court intervened in the 2000 presidential election, but this was nothing new. In fact, following that case, University of Chicago professor Cass Sunstein argued that "conservative judicial activism" is a greater threat to democracy than "liberal judicial activism" which, he predicted, would prove to be a "brief quirk of history, limited to a short time in the middle of the 20th century."[51] Nor is it clear that those with a modern liberal agenda can be consistent while promoting judicial supremacy. In doing so, they promote an anti-democratic paternalism that contemporary liberals would seemingly want to reject. If liberals are truly interested in insuring the rights of all individuals to vote, for example, why would they want to encourage the Supreme Court to overturn laws passed by elected representatives? Why give people the right to vote only to encourage the Court to ignore the will of the people voting?

In other words, judicial activism is no more necessarily a liberal position than judicial restraint is necessarily a conservative position. More importantly,

---

[51] See Cass Sunstein, *What We'll Remember in 2050*, found in E.J. Dionne Jr. and William Kristol eds. *Bush v. Gore* (Washington D.C.: Brookings Institution Press, 2001), p. 339.

judicial activism like judicial restraint, provides no legitimate judicial philosophy. In fact, today's politics give the Court no choice but an activist posture and the distinction between activists and non-activists is somewhat deceiving. Because all sides concede to the Court the power of judicial review, the Court exercises this power whether or not it actually rules on a case. By accepting a lower court's ruling, the Supreme Court in effect gives its stamp of approval. Nevertheless, some openly push for a more proactive Court and their theories must also be examined.

Activism and Democratic Theory

Among those who openly encourage the Court to play a more aggressive role in American politics are those who strongly favor democratic principles, yet see the Constitution's expression of democracy quite differently than the late Chief Justice Rehnquist did. Yale law professor Bruce Ackerman, for example, argues that the Constitution supports a "dualist" understanding of democracy. He distinguishes two levels of democratic processes in American politics. At the lower level, representatives elected according to democratic principles, make law through democratic processes. Nevertheless, because representatives sometimes represent not the voice of the American people, but the will of various special interest groups, Ackerman considers theories that make the legislative process the essence of democracy to suffer from a limited and incomplete concept of democracy.[52]

Ackerman instead argues that the Constitution does not limit democracy to the process of electing representatives. Rather, in accordance with the Preamble, he suggests that the Constitution envisions the people acting only when they adopt or amend the actual Constitution. In other words, Ackerman argues that the Constitution supports a higher form of democratic action that clearly

---

[52] See Bruce Ackerman, *Dualist Democracy The Basic Idea*, found in John H. Garvey and T. Alexander Aleinikoff, eds. *Modern Constitutional Theory: A Reader* Third Edition (St. Paul, Minnesota: West Publishing Company, 1994), p. 41.

trumps typical legislative action. For him, the people as a whole speak only during specific constitutional moments: when the Constitution was first ratified, or whenever it is amended. Ackerman supports this argument by noting that it takes a much greater effort to ratify or amend the Constitution than it does to pass a typical congressional act. Constitutional amendments require a much greater percentage of votes in both houses of Congress, and must be ratified by three fourths of the states. Typical congressional acts, on the other hand, can be passed by a simple majority in both houses and frequently have a limited appeal to groups with special interests. Consequently, normal acts of Congress often only represent the will of those groups that have made large campaign contributions, so that Congress does not speak for the people at all, but only for those who have influence in Congress.

It follows, for Ackerman, that democratic principles, far from requiring that the Court defer to Congress, in fact require the Court to protect the voice of the people, as it is reflected in the Constitution. For when acts of Congress represent special interests, only the Constitution reflects the real will of the people. Consequently, the Court champions the people's will by aggressively defending the Constitution from those in Congress who would bend it to meet the needs of special interests. Ackerman's Court thus vigorously supports democracy when it uses the Constitution to strike down congressional acts.

This argument too has merit. Constitutional amendments *do* require much greater popular support than ordinary legislation, and Congress certainly does not always represent the voice of the people. Nevertheless, this theory is also inadequate. Even if we grant Ackerman's premise that the people spoke when ratifying the Constitution (a problematic assumption at best,) there is no reason to conclude that the nine individuals sitting on the Court should have the final responsibility to determine the Constitution's meaning. And recognizing the influence of special interest groups in Congress gives no reason to believe that Court justices are above pursuing political agendas. Moreover, it would be naive to expect justices to put aside their own personal biases and look at the Constitution through purely objective lenses. Indeed, liberal critics of the majority of Supreme Court justices in the 2000 presidential case clearly doubted that the Court safeguarded the will of the people.

More importantly, Ackerman misunderstands American political mythology by reducing the Court to just another player, though perhaps an especially influential one, in the political process of determining society's values. American political culture refuses to grant this power to any messy political process or government institution. Though Ackerman is partially correct to look to the Constitution's Preamble and its emphasis on the People, American political culture actually views the People as standing self-evidently above all political institutions, including the Court and the Constitution. By allowing the Court only a typical political function, Ackerman misses this point. American political culture trusts the Court only so long as it appears aggressively to be upholding the self-evident will of the People. When the Court's actions are not self-evidently legitimate, no argument about the Court's responsibility to preserve the people's will by engaging in the political process will suffice. In other words, Ackerman is correct to understand that American political culture refuses to entrust manipulative politicians in Congress with the power to determine society's values, but he fails to comprehend that American political culture ultimately refuses to grant this power to anyone.

University of Chicago professor Cass Sunstein also argues that the Constitution promotes democratic principles. But unlike Rehnquist and Ackerman, he recognizes America's republican values as well, and argues that it is more accurate to view the Constitution as promoting "deliberative democracy" rather than mass democratic processes.[53] In other words, Sunstein does not see the Constitution as a simple framework for democracy that views elected members of Congress as promoting the will of the people. In fact, Sunstein

---

[53] See Cass R. Sunstein, *A Republic of Reasons*, found in Ibid., p. 53.

argues, the founders supported the ideal of representatives not because they favored democracy, but because they distrusted it. The founders believed that by engaging in deliberations away from the people, representatives could enact policies that would be far superior to any that the people acting as a mass could ever formulate. In short, Sunstein argues that the Constitution attempts to promote not the will of the people, but rather the superior will of those individuals who, after having participated in meaningful deliberations, best understand what is best for the people.

Sunstein justifies his argument by demonstrating that the Constitutional Convention itself was held in this tradition. The founders were confident that no good could come of a political debate completely open to the media and direct public scrutiny, and therefore held their deliberations behind closed doors. Similarly, Sunstein argues, the original Constitution intended to keep direct democracy at arm's length through such mechanisms as the Electoral College, the selection of senators by state legislatures, and indeed the life terms of the Supreme Court justices. And though Sunstein believes that Congress does have primary responsibility for making law, he further reasons that the very protection of Court members from the democratic process suggests that they too should aggressively address questions of constitutionality. This sort of action epitomizes what he sees as the deliberative ideal.

Sunstein's argument has several merits; particularly helpful is his understanding of the republican values inherent in American political culture. He aptly recognizes that those who view the Constitution as a mere framework for democracy fail to acknowledge a perennial and important side of American political culture. Furthermore, Sunstein's embracing of republican values demonstrates why judicial activism is not necessarily a liberal position. Many contemporary conservatives make similar arguments about the wisdom of keeping the demands of democracy at bay. However, by viewing the Court as just another player in the deliberative process, Sunstein makes the same mistake that

Ackerman makes. American political culture ultimately distrusts all politics, even deliberative processes. Natural law is self-evident and requires no elites deliberating in smoke-filled rooms to discover its truths. Only when the Court appears to be above politics altogether can it remain legitimate. In other words, Sunstein correctly perceives that the Court can play a legitimate role in insuring that Congress acts within proper bounds. He fails to consider that according to American political culture, the Court's role cannot be understood as political in the traditional sense. Practically, the Court may have to engage in deliberative politics. But when it appears to be just another political body, however deliberative, it loses all legitimacy.

Insuring Individual Rights Theories

Another school of thought, championed most prominently by New York University law professor Ronald Dworkin, favors a more aggressive Supreme Court, not because the Court has an integral role in the democratic process, but because the Court is necessary to protect individuals from the democratic process altogether. Dworkin sees the Constitution as embracing a theory of majority rule with minority rights, and argues that the only way to take the concept of minority rights seriously is to allow for an aggressive Supreme Court.[54] Like Rehnquist and Ely, Dworkin considers Congress to represent the will of the majority. But unlike Rehnquist and Ely, he reads the Constitution as demanding that the Court assume primary responsibility for protecting minority rights.

Dworkin's argument is based on the *liberal* assumption that government is necessary because individuals, ever partial to their own position, need an outside arbitrator. If the guarantees in the Bill of Rights are to mean anything, Dworkin reasons, the majority who make the law cannot be the same people who determine that the law is consistent with the Bill of Rights. The logic of the Bill of Rights suggests rights *against* the majority's will.

[54] See Ronald Dworkin, *Taking Rights Seriously* (Cambridge: Harvard University Press, 1972).

In other words, Dworkin argues that those who focus only on the democratic processes enshrined in the Constitution ignore not only the whole Bill of Rights, but much of American political culture as well. If individual rights are to be protected, the Court must do it. Members of Congress, like presidents, maintain their positions by pleasing the majority and cannot be expected to protect minorities. Courts alone then, can protect the rights of minorities from over-zealous democratic majorities.

Dworkin's argument also appears sound on the surface, harmonizing with the *liberal* belief in unalienable rights that must be protected from government. Furthermore, he is consistent with American political culture by viewing government as the major threat to individual rights and suggesting that rights are safe only when the people who make up the government are not the same people who protect the rights.

Nevertheless, this argument also proves inadequate on inspection, because Dworkin does not allow that individual rights are endemically in direct conflict with each other. Every individual is a potential minority, or a member, simultaneously, of many different minorities with different, even conflicting interests. It is, therefore, overly simplistic to envision a society where one minority is pitted against a unified majority. And it is not always clear whether the Court should protect the individual whose freedoms are threatened by potential government regulation, or the individual whose freedoms will be threatened without government regulation. For example, should an individual's right to privacy and reputation be protected from the overly enthusiastic journalist, or should the journalist's right to publish be protected regardless of who gets tarnished in the process? If the Court's role is to protect minority rights, which minority should it protect?

This egregious oversight is not simply Dworkin's. *Liberal* mythology assumes that individual rights can exist simultaneously without being in conflict. And it assumes that the answers to questions of conflict are self-evident to all reasonable individuals. Dworkin too seems to think that these answers are self-evident. But the controversy over the Court's rulings on so many issues suggests otherwise. For example, in 1973 it may have been self-evident to a majority of the justices on the Court that a woman has an unalienable right to choose an abortion, but this clearly was not self-evident to those who oppose the ruling.

In other words, though Dworkin correctly senses that taking rights seriously means not trusting Congress with the final say, he offers no reason to trust the Court either. He fails to recognize that once the Court enters the business of deciding which rights to protect and which to subvert, it becomes every bit as threatening to individual freedoms as Congress. Finally, though Thomas Jefferson was unwilling to wait for King George to come to his senses and recognize the unalienable rights of the colonists, he also did not look to the king's court to be the final protector of individual rights.

Conclusion

There are certainly other voices arguing over the proper role of the Court; the above analysis does not exhaust all the nuances in the many positions held. But it does reflect the primary themes of our major judicial philosophies. Their shortcomings reflect a shared weakness. All fail to fully comprehend American political culture's demand that politics refrain from determining society's values, and all insert the Court into the normal political process. Advocates of judicial restraint encourage the Court to stay out of politics unless it is clear or prudent to do otherwise, while advocates of judicial activism initially grant the Court a definite political role. Viewing the Court as another, if somewhat special, political institution, is a serious oversight. American political mythology, skeptical of politics, conceives the rights of individuals as existing independent of all political processes. Judicial activists comprehend this insofar as they give Congress no authority to trample on minority rights. Yet by reducing the Court to another political body with the power to determine which rights will and will not be protected, they ignore this most important principle. Judicial restraint theories are equally inadequate. They too wish to limit government power, but in their attempt to limit excessive Court interference, they fail to account for American political culture's restrictions on Congress's legislative powers. They error further in suggesting that the Court can enter the typical political process to correct congressional mistakes when it is clearly prudent to do so.

All of these theories deny the full richness and complexity of America's contradictory political mythology. The result is weak judicial philosophies that cannot navigate the more difficult situations. This weakness is understandable. As I argue in the first three chapters, American political culture is both complex and contradictory; desiring clarity, we easily buy into judicial philosophies that sacrifice completeness to tidiness. But, this need not be the case. The next chapter argues that directly embracing the richness of American political culture makes possible a vibrant and consistent understanding of the Court's essential role in American politics.

Knights of the Myth

Chapter Five
Preserving Myth: The Essential Role of The Supreme Court

The last chapter argued that the dominant judicial philosophies err in conceiving the Supreme Court as a typical player in America's political machinations. That is, they require members of the Court to participate in the dubious process of determining which values society will or will not enforce. In doing so, it was argued, these theories fail to acknowledge the importance of American political culture's refusal to grant any political institution the authority to make such determinations. For according to American political culture, legitimate social values derive from a mythical natural law; above all, the Court must never appear to violate this natural law. In sum, the failure to fully account for the contradicting demands of a rich American political culture prevented each theory from providing a consistent and helpful judicial philosophy.

The first three chapters of this book locate the wealth of American political mythology in the complexity of its many contradicting ideals. Chapter One showed that even as American political culture celebrates first and foremost the unalienable rights of the individual, it requires that government act to preserve those rights. This leads to contradiction; to preserve rights, government must exercise enormous powers that threaten individual liberty. Moreover, while sensible individuals are expected to compromise and submit to the will of the majority, the majority is capable of tyranny itself. As a result, the true patriot must defiantly stand against the majority when the situation demands it. Chapter One also demonstrates that American political culture has contradicting views of the Constitution. On the one hand, the Constitution is perceived as an almost sacred document handed down by wise *founding fathers* to guide America and protect it from the shortsighted and often misguided democratic process. On the other hand, the Constitution is perceived as a document in progress that the majority can amend, suggesting that the people, not the Constitution, govern.

The conflicting demands placed on government representatives are also examined in the first chapter. For even as Americans expect representatives to act paternalistically—using their privileged positions to pursue what is best for their constituents, they are also expected to respond both to the will of the majority and to the demands of individuals whose rights suffer at the hands of an intrusive majority.

Finally Chapter One examined the contradicting expectations regarding property rights. While Americans view property rights as God-given and necessary for liberty, property rights in America ultimately depend on abundance. According to American political mythology, one has a right to property only as long as all have equal rights to property, and government has an obligation to safeguard these rights for all.

Chapter Two examined the contradicting demands that America's *liberal* heritage makes on government institutions. First and foremost, *liberalism* demands that government be controlled. The assumption that "men are not angels" creates a distrust of government that underlies *liberal* philosophy. This attempt to control government involves separating state power from national power; creating separate legislative, executive, and judicial branches; sharing legislative, executive, and judicial powers; and, finally, granting majorities the power of the vote. Yet, at the same time American political mythology still envisions a natural law standing above all these institutions—making it impossible for any single government institution to legitimately claim final authority to resolve disputes between institutions, and thus creating a crisis of authority in American politics. I argued, however, that this crisis of authority is the great strength of American politics, making it virtually impossible for any government action to avoid serious criticism. Nevertheless, the practical need remains for some government institution to exercise final authority. That responsibility, I claim, has fallen to the U.S. Supreme Court, putting the Court in a real quandary: it must exercise this authority while *appearing* not to.

Finally, Chapter Three examined the contradicting demands of republicanism. Republican ideals play a crucial role in American politics by tempering the excesses of *liberal* individualism and mass democracy. Republicanism emphasizes virtue, self-sacrifice, and the public good, ideals that also run deep in American political culture. I argued that elites who powerfully influence American politics must preserve the republican ideals from constant *liberal* democratic attacks, if they are to be preserved, and that the Court has a specific and crucial responsibility in this endeavor.

To be sure, no single government institution or public initiative can assure the viability of the many contradicting ideals in American political mythology. Myth is not easily controlled, and the relationship between individuals, institutions, and ideals within a political culture is complex: influence flows in many directions, individuals are shaped by cultural expectations, and over time, political mythology evolves according to the ideas and actions of changing individuals and institutions. It would be erroneous, therefore to suggest that any institution, group, or individual is primarily responsible for maintaining American political myth. Nevertheless, mythical ideals can and do change, and those that provide an indispensable service to society ought to be protected and encouraged wherever possible.

This chapter argues that such protection and encouragement define the Supreme Court's primary role. Although attempting to preserve America's rich political culture is also a political activity, it keeps the Court above the dirty level of politics American political culture refuses to accept, *period*! To grant this as the Court's essential role, I will argue, could result in a consistent and useful standard against which to measure the Court, provide useful criteria for the selection of justices, and, most importantly, insure greater respect for the Court, which will in turn help preserve the important contradicting ideals in America's political mythology.

The Essential Role of the U.S. Supreme Court

Having inherited the power to determine the constitutionality of all laws brought before it, the Court is uniquely positioned to encourage the preservation of American mythical ideals. In fact, most constitutional questions that come before the Court involve conflicting but, from the perspective of American political culture, equally legitimate ideals. That is why parties on both sides of the issue generally feel that the Constitution, reason, or natural law support them.

Presented with such situations, the Court has the opportunity to re-emphasize the value of each ideal in question. Since the Court has the final say, all concerned eyes watch closely to see how it will resolve this clash of ideals. These situations might tempt Court members to champion one ideal over another, yet prudence demands that they resist such temptation. It is absolutely vital that, while it rejects the particular arguments a case may raise, the Court reaffirms the mythical ideals on which the arguments are based. In other words, the Court must reject arguments without rejecting ideals, a most challenging but supremely important act. The Court must extol majority rule even as it celebrates individual moral responsibility. It must praise the rule of law even as it glories in the people's right to defy law. It must exalt individual property rights even as it lauds the people's power to govern and tax. It must champion state sovereignty even as it affirms the sovereignty of the national government. In short, it must demonstrate deep and convincing respect for each of the conflicting ideals examined in the first three chapters.

To do so, justices must fully understand and accept this role, which means that those responsible for determining the membership of the Court understand

and accept it too. Thus, arguing about whether the Court should be liberal or conservative is beside the point, and diverts attention from the Court's most important obligation. America has never needed a liberal Court to right the wrongs of overly conservative legislatures, nor does America now need a conservative Court to counterbalance liberal agendas. Rather than exercising this kind of check and balance function, the Court should preserve *all* important contradicting ideals simultaneously. For only the richness of the contradiction not the swinging from one partisan pole to another insures a healthy society.

This responsibility is complicated by the fact that the Court can only accomplish it by using its political power. Thus the Court's limited exercise of power must be seen as another ideal to be balanced along with the ideals of separation of powers and legislative supremacy. Above all else, the Court must not encourage the perception that it has a political responsibility to determine which ideals are more important at any given time. All of the central ideals of American political culture outlined in previous chapters are equally important. Moreover, the Court's challenge is not a simple balancing act. *Balancing* implies compromise and misses the point. Each ideal needs preserved in its purity; mythical ideals lose their power when compromised. Unalienable rights, for example, are absolutes. You either have them or you do not. Compromise violates the integrity of the ideal. Thus the Court must not balance but juggle—keeping all essential ideals in the air at all times. It must never attempt to resolve issues once and for all. Its job is to just keep juggling.

Two primary factors determine how well the Court discharges this essential task: the logic by which the Court reaches its ruling, and the ruling itself. Generally the logic is most significant, because it reveals the extent of the Court's commitment to each ideal in question. However, sometimes the Court's ruling speaks louder than its logic. In these situations the Court's hands may be virtually tied. If, for example, accepting a case makes the Court appear to show disregard for certain ideals, its logic is irrelevant.

The following sections examine two controversial cases from this perspective: the 1973 *Roe* v. *Wade* abortion case and the more recent and highly publicized *Bush* v. *Gore* 2000 presidential election case. In each case, I will argue, the Court failed to take seriously its supreme responsibility to preserve the healthy contradictions in American political mythology. In these two cases the Court suffered from myopia—it was too caught up with immediate concerns to see the broader, more essential picture.

Roe v. *Wade*

Though generally a case's outcome matters most to the parties in question, usually the reasoning behind the outcome matters most to American society at large. Careful reasoning underscores the necessity of all legitimate ideals in question, even as it shows that all ideals may not apply equally to the particular situation. And though I argue that the Court ultimately failed to meet its most essential obligation in the controversial 1973 *Roe* v. *Wade* case, the reasoning within the case is an excellent example of deep respect for multiple ideals.

In *Roe*, one party claimed that women should be treated as mature responsible adults, not only able to make difficult medical decisions regarding their pregnancies, but with a constitutionally guaranteed right to do so. This argument rests squarely on the *liberal* myth of God-given unalienable individual rights, an ideal so fundamental to American political culture as to be inarguable. Nor is the right to make choices that deeply affect one's personal life exclusively a liberal or conservative ideal. Unless women are to be treated as second-class citizens, and thus as less-than-human, they deserve the right to determine what to do with their own lives just as much as free men do. Though the Constitution makes no mention of the right to choose an abortion, contemporary standards make it hard to argue that the Constitution requires women to subject themselves to the will of others in such matters.

The other party in *Roe* argued that state governments have a constitutionally valid responsibility to protect the health and welfare of their citizens, including the welfare of both women interested in abortions and the potential human life within the womb. This argument is also rooted in mythical ideals common to American political culture, including the perceived need for government to protect those individual rights most vulnerable to the opportunism of others. This ideal too crosses party lines. As chapters One and Three argued, even while American political mythology celebrates individual autonomy, it also embraces restricted government paternalism to thwart predatory self-interests. From this perspective, government has an obligation not only to protect the vulnerable fetus inside the womb, but also to protect women who may be particularly vulnerable due to the trauma associated with an unwanted pregnancy. This argument is thus not necessarily disrespectful of women, because it is consistent with other arguments regarding medical decisions in which men and women both are often vulnerable to the seemingly all-wise physician. Indeed, liberals and conservatives alike consider oversight of the medical profession a necessary government function.

Significantly, the party arguing for the rights of women in *Roe* did not openly deny the responsibility of states to regulate the medical profession and thus insure the health and welfare of their citizens. Nor did the party representing the state argue against the mythical ideal of unalienable rights. Neither side rejected the mythical ideals of the other. As in most constitutional cases that go before the Court, both arguments are deeply rooted in American political mythology. Rather than openly challenge fundamental political ideals, then, opposing sides simply ignore each other's claims. If it is to meet its essential responsibility, however, the Court does not have this luxury. Faced with equally valid claims, the Court must acknowledge, validate, and even celebrate both sets of *ideals* even as it rules in favor of one or the other *parties*.

Justice Harry Blackmun, who wrote the *Roe* opinion, nearly succeeded in doing this very thing. He suggests that both perspectives should be respected, that indeed the state does have a constitutional responsibility to look after the health and welfare of its citizens, including women and fetal life. Nevertheless, he reasoned, this valid concern of the state cannot completely negate a woman's constitutional right to exercise her will in this matter. To support both arguments, Blackmun developed what became the highly controversial trimester format. Blackmun reasoned that the woman's right to choose should prevail in the first trimester, when the health risks of abortion were minimal and where the chances of the fetus surviving outside the womb were negligible. As the pregnancy reached later stages, he concluded, the state interest in protecting the health of the woman increased along with the risks in having an abortion, while the state interest in protecting the life of the unborn child increased along with the child's potential viability. In sum, Blackmun argued that both claims for constitutional protection were equally valid but deserved different consideration depending on the stage of the pregnancy.

It goes without saying that Blackmun's logic has proven highly controversial. By suggesting that both positions were legitimate, *Roe* utterly failed to settle the abortion question and spawned many cases seeking further clarification from the Court. However, this should be considered the strength of Blackmun's argument, not its weakness. For even as he upheld the right for women to make important choices without government intervention, Blackmun kept alive the ideal that the state has an important responsibility to insure the health and welfare of its citizens, and kept open the possibility of considering the rights of the fetus.

In short, *Roe*'s logic deserves respect for keeping all possibilities open. Blackmun did not make compromises between the conflicting ideals. He juggled them both. He championed the woman's unalienable right to self-determination, while upholding the state responsibility to protect its citizens. These two positions cannot be compromised. The conflict between the rights of individual women and the legitimate responsibility of the state is irresolvable. Both ideals are valid in the mythical sense, and both need to be equally preserved to sustain a healthy society. It follows that constant struggle will accompany America's attempts to live with this conflict. But this is a desirable struggle, and should be celebrated.

Despite his careful logic, however, Blackmun ignored other equally important ideals, making it possible for many to perceive the *Roe* decision as a blatant power grab. Justices in the majority appeared all too willing to remove their mythical robes for personal agendas. Consequently, with *Roe* the Court ultimately failed in its primary function: preserving the guiding influence of America's vital mythical ideals. Some political situations require more from the Court than a carefully crafted opinion. *Roe* v. *Wade* was such a case.

Roe overreached. The Court went too far in rewriting American law. Prior to *Roe*, state governments assumed that the Constitution granted them unquestioned authority to regulate all medical practices within their borders. When the Court suddenly decided otherwise, several important mythical ideals were violated in a rather cavalier way, including the ideal of state sovereignty and the ideal of separation of powers. In other words, though Blackmun carefully demonstrated respect for both the autonomy of women and the state responsibility to regulate the medical profession, he demonstrated no serious commitment either to the ideal that requires the Court to refrain from making law or state sovereignty. Many perceived the Court to be acting as a super legislature in violation of constitutionally protected state authority. And, to be sure, not only does the Constitution say nothing about unalienable abortion rights, American history demonstrates that this right was not considered among the non-enumerated rights implied in the Constitution. State governments had regulated and even banned abortions from the very beginning of the nation. When the Court suddenly claimed they could no longer do so, it went too far, too fast.

Whenever Court rulings clearly change the way the Constitution is to be understood, they tread tenuous ground. When such rulings are highly controversial and arouse partisan passion, the Court is on extremely tenuous ground. And in this case, the Court was wrong—not because the right of women to choose is not legitimate, but because the Court failed to convincingly demonstrate a commitment to the other essential ideals in question. In so doing, the Court invited serious and determined criticism that over time has undermined its integrity as the non-political keepers of natural law and subsequently the precious relationship between contradicting mythical ideals and political practice. For many, the *Roe* decision demonstrated a calloused and complete disrespect for the rule of law, the separation of powers, state sovereignty, and most importantly, the sacred lives of innocent unborn babies. Blackmun's nod toward the state interest in protecting potential life came across as superficial and hypocritical. Galvanized by a sense of moral superiority based on natural law, the Court's critics dedicated themselves to overturning the decision. In fact, so obvious did the Court's political agenda appear to its critics, that *Roe* provoked an intense political backlash that, according to Alan Dershowitz, did more harm than good to the women's movement.[55]

Even more significant for our purposes than the harm done to the women's movement by *Roe* was the damage done to the role of mythical ideals in American politics. The decision failed so miserably even to *appear* to be based on more than personal opinion, that it could not garner the least amount of respect from its opponents. This is not to say that a wise Court will always command everyone's respect. But it does suggest that members of the Court must acknowledge political reality and take it under deep consideration as it deliberates.[56]

---

[55] See Alan M. Dershowitz, *Supreme Injustice*, pp. 191-197.

[56] In what has become generally known as her Madison Lecture, prior to joining the Supreme Court Justice Ginsburg argued that *Roe* went too far. Ginsburg argued that the more extreme elements of the anti-abortion law could have been struck down while leaving the more moderate

In 1973, the Court knew that the abortion question was extremely controversial; they knew that their decision would be interpreted as legislating from the bench. And though they could not foresee the degree to which their decision would be disrespected, their failure to fully grasp the political reality of their time resulted in what Dershowitz calls a cynical conservative counter offensive to pack the Court with politicos willing to do the bidding of the Republican Party in general, and overturn *Roe* in particular. Conservatives justify this extremism by arguing that since in *Roe* liberals were unwilling to require the Court to abide by neutral principles, true conservatives throughout America needed to be equally political and one sided.[57] The ideal of an objective and balanced Court has been openly discarded.[58]

Though it can be very tempting to take short cuts and impose forward-looking agendas through the brute exercise of power, the long-term success of any political policy still depends on the legitimizing role of mythical ideals. And though this frustrates those who want quick change, it postpones the dark day when ideals cease entirely to legitimize political decisions. Indeed *Roe* came about because of the power of an ideal, not because five women wanting abortions managed to take over the Court.

Whether we favor abortion rights or the current conservative agenda, when the Court becomes just another political battlefield, we all suffer. Justices must above all encourage the myth that the Court neutrally enforces justice rooted in a natural law greater than the political agendas of all factions. This obligation

---

regulations alone. She believed this would have not only been less controversial for the Court, but could have perhaps been accepted without resulting in the degree of passion against the women's right to choose which *Roe* generated. See Susan Low Bloch and Thomas G. Krattenmaker, eds. *Supreme Court Politics: The Institution and Its Procedures* (St. Paul, Minnesota: West Publishing Company, 1994,) p. 290.

[57] Ibid. Dershowitz argues that the seeds of the blatantly political power grab in the *Bush* v. *Gore* decision were originally planted by the political agendas of liberal Court justices culminating in *Roe* v. *Wade*, and argues that for the health of democracy the Court should stay out of issues better be resolved by the political process.

[58] In *The Tempting of America*, Robert Bork argues that the Court has become too involved in promoting political agendas like those pushed by the liberal Court that decided *Roe*. However, Bork seems unaware that his own nomination was part of an equally political agenda.

is greater than preserving any minority right, any state power, or even the Constitution itself. As history has shown, the Constitution can be manipulated to mean any number of things. It is only the power of America's conflicting political ideals that makes appealing to the Constitution meaningful.

In sum, as important as it may have seemed to the Court that the country treat women as capable adults with equal rights, it was more important that the country continue to believe in its political ideals. In the end, all appeals to liberty (particularly those of women and any other group not at the center of power) depend on faith in these ideals, with all their rich contradictions. By using their positions to promote a single important ideal at the expense of the bundle of contradicting ideals, Blackmun and the justices who joined him, failed to meet their essential responsibility.

Bush* v. *Gore

Similarly, the five members on the Rehnquist Court who made up the majority in the 2000 presidential election case could not rule in favor of George W. Bush without appearing to pursue personal political agendas. They too must have known this, and so should not have succumbed to temptation. This is true regardless of what the Florida State Supreme Court had done. Their responsibilities as members of the U.S. Supreme Court do not vanish because another court is blatantly political. In fact, because the Florida court had already been accused of partisan politics, it was vitally important that the U.S. Supreme Court not be. In this politically charged atmosphere, the Court needed at all costs to salvage the legal system's integrity. It would have helped had they simply refused to hear the case, thus demonstrating their commitment to judicial principles even at the risk of losing the presidency to a Democratic candidate they clearly did not favor. By stopping the Florida court-ordered recount and eventually ruling in favor of George W. Bush, they did just the opposite. In effect they admitted that they were as political as some of their most vocal critics had previously feared, that they were as political as the liberal justices they had so consistently condemned.

As stated above, to live up to their essential responsibility, Supreme Court justices must first and foremost make sure that they do not *appear* to be just another political body. Of course, the Court cannot help but engage in politics; because it is expected to have the final say on questions of constitutionality, it unavoidably helps determine what values American society will enforce. Had the Court refused to hear *Bush* v. *Gore*, it would have exercised political power. But justices can do much to insure that the Court does not *appear* to be motivated by personal or partisan politics. For instance they can recognize how their actions will be perceived in the political circumstances of the time. In *Bush*, the justices made it *appear* that they were governed not by principles, but by the raw power of their position on the Court. Given the politics of the day, they simply could not rule in favor of George W. Bush without appearing personally motivated.

In fact, the majority in the *Bush* v. *Gore* decision arguably exceeded that in *Roe* v. *Wade* in blatantly appearing to promote their political agendas. The majority in *Roe* had previously established a pattern of using the equal protection clause of the Fourteenth Amendment to broaden individual freedoms and overturn state laws. Though with *Roe* they went too far, at least the justices in the majority were consistent with their previous rulings and logic. But as every serious Court watcher knows, prior to *Bush* v. *Gore*, the five majority justices demonstrated a clear disdain for equal protection arguments as a tool to weaken state sovereignty. In fact, one of the defining characteristics of a "conservative" justice is to avoid over reliance on the equal protection clause. The distilled essence of liberal jurisprudence, in the minds of most conservatives, is the willingness to make equal protection arguments exactly like the one made by the majority in *Bush* v. *Gore*.

Nor are the four dissenting justices beyond reproach. This is not because they should have ruled against the Florida Supreme Court in order to remain consistent with their own established jurisprudence. Justices, Stevens, Souter, Ginsburg, and Breyer, could vote to let the Florida Supreme Court decision stand and be consistent with their more liberal leanings, as the lower court's ruling demanded Florida votes be counted. Rather, their dissenting opinions sidestepped their obligation to preserve the integrity of American political ideals. Knowing that the majority justices were going to be perceived as extremely, even illegitimately, political in voting for George W. Bush, and knowing that the majority was going to vote the way it did regardless of any minority protests, these justices could have found the courage to set aside their personal resentment at the majority's audacity, and limited the potential damage. *Bush* v. *Gore* needed a unanimous opinion to carry any moral weight with potential critics. As wrong as the five majority justices were to ignore their own precedents and the realities of the political situation, the four dissenters only made things worse with their dissents. In *Bush* v. *Gore*, none of the justices lived up to the Court's essential role of preserving the power of American political mythology.

One final point: though some might argue, as I did in Chapter Three, that it is possible that the majority acted in good conscience on the republican ideal whereby elites must preserve the nation from itself, the majority still failed to meet its essential responsibility. To be sure, the republican ideal demands that individuals sometimes sacrifice even the appearance of personal integrity for the good of the nation, and majority justices perhaps believed they were doing just that. We can never know. But even if we give them that benefit of doubt, even if we assume that they knew their reliance on the Fourteenth Amendment would be perceived as hypocritical, we still cannot let them off the hook for failing to meet their primary obligation of safeguarding American idealism. American mythology has elements of both republicanism and *liberalism*. And just as the Court in *Roe* had a greater responsibility than preserving the minority rights of women, so too the Court in *Bush* v. *Gore* had a greater responsibility than settling the immediate question. Republican paternalism must be used with great caution.

Preserving it is much more important than determining who should occupy the U.S. presidency.

The Court and the Realm of Myth

Chapter Four demonstrated the inadequacy of judicial theories that fail to comprehend the mythical demands of American political culture. By claiming that justices should adhere to the founder's intent unless prudence demands otherwise, original intent theorists ultimately encourage justices to descend into the messy political process. Theories recommending that justices defer to Congress unless Congress clearly errors similarly endorse Court involvement in dirty political machinations. Both these theories ignore the long tradition in American political culture that refuses to grant unlimited political authority to any government body, including Congress or the Court. Theories that call for a more aggressive Court prove equally problematic. Those that emphasize protecting minority rights fail to determine which minority needs protection, because every individual is a potential minority. A justice committed to protecting individuals from the majority must ultimately either rule against every government action that can be construed as having a negative affect on any individual, or, once again, engage the Court in the political process of determining which of the many competing interests will receive the government's blessing.

But if we understand the Court's primary role as preserving American political mythology, these problems vanish. Though universal acceptance of this standard would not end all controversy, it would substantially re-establish a meaningful, consistent purpose for the Court, do much to insure freedom, and provide useful guidance to justices in the tough cases they are called on to resolve. As we have seen, American political ideals are at once too fundamental to a healthy democracy and too contradictory for meaningful compromises in any given situation. The ideals do their best work in their pure form. The *liberal* ideal of unalienable individual rights must remain pure even in the face of the limits on freedom government actually requires. Similarly the ideals of federalism, balance of powers, and separation of powers must remain pure in the face of actual practice that demands a blurring of powers and boundaries to be effective. In short, even though none of these ideals can be realized in practice, they provide indispensable goals for personal and social aspiration; we must believe in the inviolable purity of these ideals, and seek to realize them even though practice demands that we never do.

Moreover, the power of judicial review itself is a mythical ideal. It is no wonder that constitutional scholars have failed to make a consistent logical argument for its use. Mythical ideals are not logically consistent. As noted in Chapter Two, the founders did not explicitly grant the Court judicial review, to do so would severely weaken the separation of powers principle. Yet as also noted, the mythical ideal of natural law superseding all acts of Congress requires the Court to exercise this power, and it only follows that the Court's primary responsibility when exercising judicial review involves preserving the very myth on which it is based.

In other words, asking the Court to preserve our political ideals is to ask it to operate in the realm of myth. And though this too would engage the Court in politics, it is a higher politics; a politics American political culture not only demands from the Court, but a politics the Court is most suited for. Black robes, secrecy, disconnection from the democratic process, all serve to add mystique and mystery to the Court. As long as justices recognize that no resolution to any particular case is as important as the larger issue of preserving the power of the ideal, it can meet this essential responsibility.

Most importantly, Supreme Court justices must be critically aware of political realities. Not that they must bow to expectations of the democratic processes, but the opposite. They must avoid the very appearance of engaging in normal politics, which requires that they be sensitive to how their actions can and will be perceived by the watching public. Justices must recognize the times when the only way to transcend politics as usual requires either refusing to get involved or ruling a certain way. A responsible justice must take the pulse of American politics and recognize the immediate limits political pressures place on the Court. Justices who appear to have a partisan ideology have betrayed their charge.

A brief examination of the historic *Brown* v. *Board of Education* demonstrates this point. Like *Roe*, *Brown* controversially overturned a history of precedent cases, stepped into a traditional arena of state power, and ruled on an inflammatory issue. Unlike *Roe,* however, *Brown* commanded respect from all sides and continues to be seen as a high point for the Court.

From the perspective of those wishing to end racial segregation in schools, *Brown* was the perfect example of the Court making lemonade out of the lemons of historical precedent and legislative practice. For example, in the now infamous *Plessy* v. *Ferguson* decision, when it upheld Louisiana's law requiring racial segregation on separate but equal grounds, the Court justified itself by invoking the common and unquestioned practice of racial segregation in schools. In his opinion, Justice Brown noted that school segregation based on race was a common practice even in states "where the political rights of the colored race have been longest and most earnestly enforced." He further noted that Congress itself had enacted legislation regarding segregation in schools in the District of Columbia.

Ironically, however, in *Brown* v. *Board of Education* the separate but equal ideal espoused in *Plessy* and reinforced by years of jurisprudence gave Chief Justice Warren the very key he needed to successfully rule against state supported school segregation without appearing overtly political. Rather than openly challenging state authority to make school policy and thereby engaging in the regular political process, Warren could focus on an ideal from the Court's own previous rulings. Significantly, Warren could ask if the Court (not states) had gotten it right in the past. Was the Court's own standard of separate but equal really working? Could it ever work? By focusing attention on a standard the

Court itself had established, Warren successfully dodged a direct confrontation with the ideal of state sovereignty and thus appeased the mythical demand that the Court stay out of politics.

Warren further demonstrated his understanding of the political realities the Court faced by his care in not stepping on any toes unnecessarily. He recognized the importance of not going too far too fast. As Richard Kluger argues in *Simple Justice*, "The opinion [of Chief Justice Warren] ... walked the tightrope between acknowledging the relevance of community attitudes and yielding to them the right to delay the exercise of anybody's constitutional rights." Kluger further notes: "The Court did not fix a date for the end of segregation, as Thurgood Marshall had so vigorously requested. ... And by almost any measure, it gave the South a great deal more of what it had asked at the final round of arguments than it gave to the Negro."[59]

To be sure, the Court's ruling in *Brown* did not once and for all end racial segregation in American schools. Yet it did champion the ideal of equality that continues to inform American policies. Because of the ideals espoused in *Brown*, it became harder to promote racism through law. Moreover, *Brown* is generally considered a high point in the Court's history even though the Court in effect legislated from the bench, ruled against a long-standing and widely practiced tradition, and violated a previously unquestioned state prerogative. In *Brown* the Court dutifully preserved American myth by carefully juggling the competing ideals of separation of powers and state sovereignty while simultaneously nudging the country in a new direction by appealing to the ideal of individual liberty.

The Court also got it right in *Marbury* v. *Madison*, where it first relied on the mythical ideal of judicial review. Though professors of constitutional law can only with difficulty get today's students to appreciate how radical the exercise of this power is, as late as 1808 it was so controversial that the Ohio legislature

---

[59] Richard Kluger, *Simple Justice: The History of Brown v. Board of Education and Black America's Struggle for Equality* (New York: Alfred A. Knopf, 1976), p. 745.

impeached judges for voiding its legislation.[60] Ironically, however, the political circumstances surrounding *Marbury* virtually demanded Chief Justice Marshall to rely on judicial review. Fearing that President Jefferson had no intention of honoring a Court ordered *writ of mandamus*, Marshall could avoid an ugly political showdown only by refusing to exercise a power Congress had granted the Court with the Judiciary Act of 1789.

Marshall's resolution of *Marbury* proved a brilliant political move. And though he may have simply been avoiding personal and institutional embarrassment,[61] it was his political savvy that kept the Court's integrity in tact and gave birth to the ideal of judicial review.

Conclusion

If the Court is to embrace its essential role of preserving our political mythology, those involved in the appointment of justices must believe that it is in their interest to nominate and approve individuals committed to this perspective. Politically, this will be difficult, since myopic election concerns seem to demand otherwise. Furthermore, to argue openly that justices should uphold a mythical natural law would be political suicide. Even as our political culture demands it, Americans think we are too sophisticated to rely on anything as nebulous as natural law. Nevertheless, isolated from the noise of politics, Democrats and Republicans alike should find this ideal quite appealing. Both have a long-term interest in developing a Court that sees its essential role as preserving the powerful influence of contradicting ideals in American political culture.

To begin with, such a Court would do much to strengthen the *republican* ideal. As I argued in Chapter Three, excessive *liberal* individualism at times

---

[60] See James Bradley Thayer, *The Origin and Scope of the American Doctrine of Constitutional Law*, found in Walter F. Murphy et. al., *American Constitutional Interpretation*, Third Edition (New York: Foundation Press 2003), p. 673.

[61] John A. Garraty suggests that Marshall made a mistake in pushing to hear the *Marbury* v. *Madison* case and pictures Marshall as weaseling out of a corner he had painted himself into. See *Quarrels That Have Shaped the Constitution* (New York: Harper and Row 1962).

threatens to unravel the nation. Republican Party conservatives badly under-recognize their own ideological roots by arguing that the Court should defer to democratic processes. Republican ideals temper *liberal* individualism by encouraging virtues of patriotic self-sacrifice. Furthermore, republican ideals demand that elites accept the primary responsibility to promote national unity. As the Enron scandal shows, excessive *liberal* individualism among today's elites threatens America much more than their excessive paternalism.

Today's liberals should also view the Court as the great preserver of America's ideals. *Liberalism* has always relied on the power of its ideal as opposed to brute force. Thomas Jefferson legitimized the cause of individual freedom by appealing to God-given rights. And as the aftermath of *Roe* suggests, when liberals enlist the Court in power politics to promote their immediate interests, they ultimately undermine the very power of the *liberal* ideal. Liberals would do well to remember that when all becomes fair in judicial warfare, historical minorities are most likely to suffer. *Liberalism's* greatest power is the power of its ideals.

In 1990, after the Senate had refused to appoint him to the Supreme Court, Robert Bork vented his frustration in *The Tempting of America: The Political Seduction of the Law*, by arguing that politics had corrupted the judicial branch. Alan Dershowitz similarly condemns the Supreme Court's "power grab" in *Bush* v. *Gore*. From opposite ends of America's political spectrum, Bork and Dershowitz recognize that America suffers when the Court behaves as just another political body. What is really at stake is American idealism. If the Court shrinks from preserving our political mythology, the ability of ideals to provide meaningful guidance is truly in jeopardy.

What most disturbed Court watchers about *Bush* v. *Gore* was not the actual ruling, but the majority justices' sudden and arguably feigned commitment to the equal protection clause.[62] With Kennedy, O'Connor, Thomas and Scalia at his side, Chief Justice Rehnquist seemed willing to deny the Court's essential duty. He implied that ideals do not matter, that all we really have is power politics.

Ironically, then, Court justices can meet their essential responsibility only by personally resisting the individualism *liberal* theory extols. Court justices cannot succumb to the *liberal* encouragement to use power to promote individual agendas. To succeed in their role, they must judiciously adopt the republican ideal of virtue. In other words, *liberalism* can only survive when accompanied by a competing and contradicting republican ideal. As shown in Chapter Three, the founders seemed to know this, at least subconsciously; they believed that good government required virtuous individuals in key positions of power. Unchecked *liberal* individualism will destroy itself.

In short, though some may think it wishful thinking to ask Court justices to exhibit extraordinary fortitude and selflessness, to give up on republican virtue ultimately means giving up on *liberalism* too. We might as well proclaim that only power matters and that the American ideal of *liberal* freedom is mere fantasy. But, we do not think it utopian foolishness to ask soldiers to give their lives for America. We still celebrate firefighters and police officers who risk everything in the line of duty. In short, American idealism continues to matter. If we wish this to remain so, Democrats and Republicans alike would do well to recognize the need for a Court devoted to mythical ideals and wary of blatant political wrangling. Both parties need to seriously reconsider the symbolism of Lady Justice. While the scales she holds symbolizes the compromises necessary to mete out justice between various interests, her blindfold symbolizes the mythical need to appear impartial and above politics as she does so.

---

[62] See E.J. Dionne Jr. and William Kristol, eds., *Bush* v. *Gore: The Court Cases and the Commentary* (Washington D.C: The Brookings Institution, 2001).

Selected Bibliography

Bailyn, Bernard. *The Ideological Origins of the American Revolution*. Cambridge: Harvard University Press. 1967.

Boorstin, Daniel. *The Genius of American Politics*. Chicago: The University of Chicago Press. 1953.

Bork, Robert H. *The Tempting of America: The Political Seduction of the Law*. New York: The Free Press. 1990.

Brison, Susan J. and Sinnott-Armstrong, Walter. Eds. *Contemporary Perspectives on Constitutional Interpretation*. Boulder: Westview Press 1993.

Carr, Edward Hallett. *The Twenty Years' Crisis 1919-1939: An Introduction to the Study of International Relations*. London: MacMillan and Co. LTD, New York: St. Martin's Press. 1962.

Cronin, T. "Resurgent Congress and the Imperial Presidency," *Political Science Quarterly*. 95 (Summer, 1980): 209-37.

Dershowitz, Alan M. *Supreme Injustice: How the High Court Hijacked Election 2000.* Oxford, New York: Oxford University Press 2001.

Dewey, John. *The Public and its Problems*. Athens: Swallow Press/Ohio University Press. 1927.

Dionne, E.J. Jr. and Kristol, William. Eds. *Bush V. Gore*. Washington D.C.: Brookings Institution Press. 2001.

Dworkin, Ronald. *A Matter of Principle*. Cambridge: Harvard University Press. 1985.

Dworkin, Ronald. *Taking Rights Seriously*. Cambridge: Harvard University Press. 1972.

Ely, John Hart. *Democracy and Distrust: A Theory of Judicial Review*. Cambridge: Harvard University Press, Third Printing 1980.

Garraty, John A. *Quarrels That Have Shaped the Constitution*. New York: Harper and Row 1962.

Garvey, John H., Aleinikoff, T. Alexander. Eds. *Modern Constitutional Theory: A Reader* Third Edition. St. Paul, Minnesota: West Publishing Company. 1994.

Hartz, Louis. *The Liberal Tradition in America*. New York: Harcourt Brace & World, Incorporated. 1955.

Hirschman, Albert O. *The Passions and the Interests: Political Arguments for Capitalism Before Its Triumph*. Princeton: Princeton University Press. 1977.

Kluger, Richard. *Simple Justice: The History of Brown v. Board of Education and Black America's Struggle for Equality.* New York: Alfred A. Knopf. 1976.

Locke, John. *The Second Treatise of Government.* New York: The Liberal Arts Press. 1952.

MacIntyre, Alasdair. *After Virtue: A Study in Moral Theory.* Notre Dame: University of Notre Dame Press. 1981.

Machiavelli, Niccolo. *The discourses.* New York: Penguin Books. 1970

Marx, Karl. *The Economic and Philosophic Manuscripts of 1844.* New York: International Publishers. 1964.

Marx, Leo. *The Machine in the Garden: Technology and the Pastoral Ideal in America.* London: Oxford University Press. 1964.

McCann, Michael W., Houseman, Gerald L. Eds. *Judging the Constitution: Critical Essays on Judicial Lawmaking.* Glenview, Illinois: Scott, Foresman and Company. 1989.

McGinness, Joe. *The Selling of The President 1968.* New York: Trident Press. 1969.

Mill, John Stuart. *On Liberty.* Indianapolis: The Bobbs-Merrill Company, Inc. 1983.

Murphy, Walter F., Fleming, James E., Barber, Sotirios A., Macedo, Stephen. Eds. *American Constitutional Interpretation.* New York: Foundation Press. 2003.

Plato, *The Republic.* Translated by Grube, G. M. A. Indianapolis: Hackett Publishing Company. 1974.

Postman, Neil. *Amusing Ourselves to Death: Public Discourse in the Age of Show Business.* New York: Penguin Books. 1985.

Perry, Barbara A. *The Priestly Tribe: The Supreme Court's Image In The American Mind.* Westport: Praeger Publishers. 1999.

Roelofs, H. Mark. *The Poverty of American Politics: A Theoretical Interpretation.* Philadelphia: Temple University Press. 1992.

Smith, Adam. *An Inquiry into the Nature and Causes of the Wealth of Nations.* London: Methuen and Co., Ltd., ed. Edwin Cannan, 1904. Fifth edition.

Wasby, Stephen L., et. al. *Desegregation from Brown to Alexander: An Exploration of Supreme Court Strategies.* Carbondale and Edwardsville: Southern Illinois University Press. 1977.

Wills, Garry. *A Necessary Evil: A History of American Distrust of Government.* New York: Simon & Schuster. 1999.

Index